UP OOR CLOSE

Memories of Domestic Life in Glasgow Tenements, 1910-1945
Jean Faley

7

The Springburn Museum Trust and White Cockade
Publishing gratefully acknowledge a generous contribution
towards the production costs of this book from
William Teacher and Sons Ltd,
whose firm was associated with Springburn
between 1961 and 1988.

1. Wilhemina Lister in the 1930s.

UP OOR CLOSE

Memories of Domestic Life in Glasgow Tenements, 1910-1945
Jean Faley

White Cockade
in association with
Springburn Museum Trust

Published by

White Cockade Publishing
71 Lonsdale Road
Oxford OX2 7ES
Tel. 01865 510411
www.whitecockade.co.uk

in association with

The Springburn Museum Trust, Glasgow

British Library Cataloguing-in-Publication Data

A catalogue record for this book is available from the British Library.

ISBN 0 9513124 5 6 paperback

Editing and text design by Perilla Kinchin
Cover design by Gerald Cinamon
Typeset in Monotype Photina at the Oxford University Computing Service
Printed in and bound in Great Britain by The Alden Press Ltd, Oxford

Front cover: Mrs Thomas in her kitchen in Gourlay Street in the 1930s.
(Photograph by John Thomas, Springburn Museum Trust)
Back cover: Jean Faley in the room of her house in Gourlay Street in the 1950s.
(Photograph by Jack McGunnigle)

For my youngest daughter,
Kathryn Grace, whose birth made this
book both necessary and possible.

Jean V. L. Hector Faley, born in 1942, was raised in Glasgow, from which she was an unwilling emigrant at the age of sixteen. She now lives with her husband, two daughters and six cats in the United States, where she is a Professor of Sociology at the University of Wisconsin. Her academic interests lie chiefly in women's studies and the sociology of medicine; she has a private interest in homoeopathy. She now tries to spend as much time as possible in Scotland, and loves talking to older people.

The Cross, Springburn

2. Springburn Cross early this century, showing
tenements integrated with shops. Note the hand-pushed milk
churn next to the tram, and the 'high back', the drying area for
the neighbouring tenement, on top of the flat-roofed shops.

Contents

Contributors with Year of Birth

James Baxter, 1926
Margaret Burniston, 1919
Margaret Burnside, 1915
Joseph Cairns, 1905
Cathy Craig, 1922
John Craig, 1924
William Dewar, 1924
John Dowie, 1906
Tommy Doyle, 1921
Hannah Fletcher, 1920
Jean Hanton, 1919
S. Graham Hoey, 1922
Dick Johnstone, 1917
James Kinnear, 1924
Betty Knox, 1922
Marion Law, 1910
Robert Lister, 1923
Agnes Lowther, 1913
Charles McCaig, 1917
Agnes McDonald, 1909
Bobby McGee, 1919
William McGinlay, 1914
Alec McGregor, 1926
Cathy McIlroy, 1918
John McKee, 1910
John McKinnon, 1922
Douglas McMillan, 1924

Martha MacMillan, 1910
Isabel Miller, 1915
Annie Miller, 1921
Agnes Muirhead, 1918
Amelia Newton, 1925
Thomas Orr, 1920
Jean Parker, 1926
Margaret Patrick, 1923
Margaret Peterson, 1921
Mary Preece, 1919
Catherine Richardson, 1915
Peter Russell, 1926
Marion Smith, 1906
Betty Smith, 1925
Henry Stewart, 1929
Jemima Stronach, 1905
Andrew Stuart, 1926
Margaret Suttie, 1920
Peggy Taylor, 1904
Mary Tourish, 1914
Mary Urquhart, 1915
†James Vaughan, 1909
Dorothy Wardynec, 1918
Sam Watt, 1919
Mary Williamson, 1922
John Wotherspoon, 1920
Ina Wotherspoon, 1924

Preface and Acknowledgements

I grew up in a tenement house in Glasgow after the Second World War. At the age of sixteen, in 1958, I was taken away unwillingly to the United States, and except for short visits and a teaching stint for six months in Scotland, I have lived there since that time, though at bottom I long still to return to live in Scotland.

I was not brought up by my parents and so my physical surroundings, friends, and close community were very important to me. Our room-and-kitchen tenement house was cosy, clean and pretty. At night, in my little recessed bed 'ben the room', I was lulled asleep by the sounds of the steam trains passing, the tinkling chimes of the Westminister clock, and the flames of the fire flickering on the wall. Over the years I have returned again and again in my mind's eye to that room, and the old kitchen with the big black fire, the recessed bed with its pretty rose coloured bedspread and matching curtains, the sideboard with its doilies and ornaments, and the little gong rather grandly used to summon visitors from the room to tea in the kitchen on a Sunday afternoon.

Ours was a well-regulated and orderly life. We lived by the horns which went off three times a day to signal the workman's daily schedule. Breakfast, dinner and tea were served more or less at the same time every day. These daily rituals, and weekly traditions – going to the pictures on a Friday night, turn- about visiting at the weekend with aunties and uncles – gave security and rhythm to the life of a child.

The close was another little world with its neat landings and stairs. Several of my friends lived there, two across the landing and two directly underneath me. The physical nearness of wee pals in the close and the back court gave the feeling of an extended family, securely there despite the inevitable falling out and making up. Neighbours were quiet and mostly friendly to close children. One in particular I remember made toffee apples: she would hear us coming up the stair and stick her head out: 'Would ye like a wee toffee apple? There ye are, dear.' On a rainy day we would sit on the stairs and play house, or tram car, or swap Victorian scraps to make sets.

There was a clannish identity derived from staying 'up oor close' or being from 'oor back', a feeling of belonging, that was very satisfying to a child. Of course we had our bullies and our 'crabbit' tenants; there was the occasional drunk or seedy character encountered in the close. But for all that, it was a much safer and freer life for a child's comings and goings. Neighbours and shopkeepers knew you by name and there was a definite sense of belonging to a community.

In many ways, then, mine was a typical tenement upbringing, representative of the majority of working-class tenement families. Not the merchant or University class in their large mansion-like tenements, not the poorer working class who knew real destitution. Even as children, we were aware that our families were hard working, clean and respectable. Cleanliness really was the key to self-esteem: 'Ma knickers are clean so they're fit tae be seen' was the crushing retort if our skirts flew up while we were playing. The value placed on neatness has left me forever in love with polished shoes, and a methodically run house, though I have to say that I often fall short of my ideal in daily life!

This long preamble is an attempt to explain to the reader why I, like the contributors to this book, treasure the memories of tenement life and its friendliness, and why over the years, I have always been drawn back to the 'something' that I could hardly put into words. Eventually, I realised that I badly wanted to retrieve and record this aspect of my past.

I came back in 1981 unprepared for the terrible shock of what Glasgow had suffered in the zeal of 'slum clearance'. In my own area of Springburn, my building had been torn down. But at least my little school and the library were still there.

It was six more years before I returned again, determined to track down old friends and perhaps their parents in the hopes that I could interview them and write about life 'Up Oor Close'. I discovered to my delight that in 'my' old library, a community museum, the Springburn Museum Trust, had been set up only the year before. Some young people had interviewed older people from Springburn tenements and there was a great deal of material waiting to be put together into a coherent form. So my original project was converted into working on the material so fortuitously to hand.

I have found reading, editing, and working with these oral histories absolutely fascinating, and have gained a great deal from this project. Not only did it assuage a deep-seated grief that had never been resolved, it gave me a sense of personal history, and a knowledge of my commmunity roots that I never had before. I discovered that Marion Smith, one of the chief contributors to this book, had lived in the same tenement building, had back-court concerts in the same back court as I – she during the First World War, I after the Second. Again and again when reading her narrative or listening to her talk I had a sense of déja vu. I was amazed and fascinated. I felt as if I was reaching across the years and touching a hand, a living hand that had touched the same bannisters, played the same games, gone to the same two schools, and loved the same library. Talking for example about the library and its guardian, she said 'And you always had to show her your hands to see if they were clean. And if they weren't, home you went to wash them before you could come back. Oh, she was awfully strict.' What?! I remembered exactly the same thing some forty years later: 'Show me your hands. And the backs!' I wondered for a brief minute if it could possibly have been the same librarian I had stood before, absolutely terrified that my hands weren't clean enough.

Time and time again I was struck by this great continuity of experience, not only with Marion Smith but with countless others too. I realise that I left Springburn just as this continuity, which was so marked in the first half of this century, was breaking down. This book then is the more precious, a tribute to very positive aspects of the old way of life in the tenements.

And so I would like to express my great personal as well as professional debt to all the contributors who have not only given of their time and memories to preserve the history of domestic tenement life for those who will come after, but have given me a wonderful experience in working on what has turned into the first of three books.

I am particularly indebted to Marion Smith whose original oral history opened a new dimension for me in this project, and who kindly recorded more memories for me via the telephone. Peggy Taylor, who lived in Possilpark, has also given me hours of her time dealing with what must have seemed like inane questions and giving me some more wonderful stories. Many other people have responded to letters, sent photographs, invited me for tea and more oral histories and talked to me on the buses; among these Aileen Nash deserves a special mention. So many people have made it possible for me to undertake this work that it is impossible to thank them all by name. I only hope that this book will be an adequate thank you.

We all owe a great debt to the Chair and Members of the Springburn Museum Trust, who worked so long to make the Museum possible, and have been so generous with access to its archives. Very special thanks must go to Mark O'Neill, the curator at the time, who one day on the steps of the museum casually said, 'Why not write a book?' His tireless encouragement, help and contribution of ideas were all above and beyond the call of duty. The other staff at the Museum, especially Susan Scott, who has helped so much with the pictures, but also Eileen Gordon and Siobhan Kirrane, know how much they too have contributed. I am very grateful to them and to all the voluntary staff of the Museum. In addition I thank Alison Lindsay at Strathclyde Regional Archives, Joe Fisher at the Mitchell Library, Glasgow, Dr Nicholas Morgan of the University of Glasgow, Lorna Hepburn at the Scottish National Trust's Tenement House, Dr Laura Quinn, Claire Hove, Shirley Bouchard and Ewen Bowie.

I am deeply grateful to Perilla Kinchin of White Cockade Publishing for her wonderful work in editing my often rambling style of writing, as well as her knowledge of Glasgow's cultural history, and insightful approach to the oral history material itself. In addition to this the sharing of boundless enthusiasm and a new friendship made the last frantic days of getting the book ready for print pleasurable and satisfying.

I thank the University of Wisconsin, River Falls for allowing me sabbatical leave and an additional leave of absence to work on this project, and also the members of the Department of Sociology who have kindly made accommodations in teaching schedules to afford me this opportunity. In particular I thank Dr John Hamman and Dr Clyde Curry Smith for collegial encouragement and support, and Dr Constantina Safilios-Rothschild, my doctoral mentor, who taught me diligence in working with thousands of pages of literature. Going further back I thank Miss Smith, Miss Sutherland and Mr Yeudall, teachers at Gourlay Street School, Springburn, Glasgow, who gave me an educational grounding to which I constantly look back with gratitude.

Warm thanks to my uncle Jack McGunnigle who once took pictures of my toys, and to my cousin George Wylie, who knows all the streets of Glasgow and gave much practical help and good-humoured encouragement. And a special place for my Midlothian family, the Wrens, who give us a loving home whenever we come to Scotland: I thank Lucy Wren for a healing friendship and David, a lover of Glasgow, for all his enthusiasm. Last but most importantly, I thank my eldest daughter Sally, who has spent hours and hours gladly and patiently looking after my youngest daughter, and giving constant encouragement in times of despair. And my husband John, who not only did most of the cooking and home upkeep, but listened to hours of talk during my obsession with the oral histories, and waded through literally hundreds of pages of my first drafts, carefully editing, and lifting my spirits with a very good imitation of Glaswegian solaces such as 'Whit's the matter, hen, huv ye lost yer scone?'

Jean Hector Faley

Department of Sociology
University of Wisconsin, River Falls, WI 54022

routines and relationships of life in the tenements. It emerges that it was the way these houses were lived in that mattered. Such housing conditions are intolerable today, but again and again these narratives recall family life lived respectably, cosily, happily in such circumstances. The nostalgia pervading them is nostalgia for a family closeness and neighbourliness which is perceived as very valuable. Such strong community feeling was a response to the harsh economic conditions under which these families lived, and was clearly enhanced by the layout of the buildings.

It is fashionable to dismiss nostalgia as some sort of indulgence, but this is too easy a response to a complex set of feelings which are in many ways like those of emigrants thinking of their country of origin. For Glaswegians over fifty (or even forty) their city has changed almost as much as if they had moved to Chicago, with the difference that there was no expectation of great change based on a decision they made themselves. None of the interviewees would deny that they have lived through hard, often grim, times, and are proud of their resilience. Their nostalgia may be pleasurable, but it is often, as the Greek root of the word suggests, a painful longing to return to a place where they feel they belong. There is a strong sense of loss, which is not unmixed with anger, arising as it does from the destruction of a way of life without people being able to choose which elements of it they would have liked to preserve. It is natural to dwell on things which were valued and have been lost, to return in the mind and conversation to once loved places and times. Nostalgic feelings are an escape from the present, but on them can be built a critique of the present, an attempt to understand why changes have taken place, an exploration of the possibility of salvaging cherished values, an argument for greater control over the way things are.

The main focus of these narratives is Springburn, a town which sprang up around the great locomotive works in the mid nineteenth century. In 1911 Springburn and neighbouring Cowlairs had the highest proportion of two-room tenement houses of any Glasgow wards, 58.5% and 58.6% respectively, reflecting the concentration here of skilled workers. The proportion of single-ends in Springburn at this time was 27.7%. At the beginning of the period covered by this book therefore, 86.2% of Springburn's homes were one- or two-room houses.

Springburn then is a part of Glasgow which is typical of the whole in its housing, as in a number of other ways. It grew very rapidly as a direct consequence of the industrial revolution; it established a community which felt itself to have a historic identity within two or three generations; it relied on a narrow range of heavy industry, which was extremely vulnerable to slumps and structural shifts in the international economy. Springburn is also like Glasgow in being widely perceived to have begun to decline in the 1960s. In fact the underlying trend had been downward throughout the period covered by this book. Glasgow shipbuilding reached a peak, never to be matched again, in 1913; Springburn built its record annual total of steam locomotives in 1905. Heavy industrial output declined not only in absolute but in relative terms, as competition from other countries such as Germany and America intensified. This long-term trend was masked by two world wars, which involved massive production of armaments followed by booms of rebuilding. The wars delayed investment in new technology, and the slumps which followed the short-lived booms were interpreted as being part of the trade cycle, rather than symptoms of deeper change in the economy.

However by the 1960s, with unemployment, decay and vandalism endemic, Springburn was clearly identified as a problem area, and like other such parts of Glasgow it was virtually destroyed. This may seem like a single act of destruction, but it was carried out in stages. The first came with the post-war re-housing programmes and the overspill policy of the 1950s, designed to relieve over-crowding and provide adequate living conditions. The planners had the best intentions but limited vision. It would seem from their actions that they did not think that urban communities existed – a common assumption based on the idea that communities were found in the country, not in the impersonal city; and that people (or 'labour' as they were known) were, or should be, mobile, as middle class people were. There were studies which revealed the high quality of some aspects of urban community life, but these were voices of dissent which stand out more in retrospect than they did at the time, when new building technologies seemed to offer the solution to intractable historic problems. Dispersing people to new towns and housing schemes was seen as a logistical, not a cultural problem. The tenements left behind by the people began to decay.

The town planners then were responsible for the first stage of the destruction of Springburn. They got the tower-blocks and deck-access schemes built and the derelict factories cleared. The second phase was brought about by the transport planners. They designed the road which cuts through where Springburn used to be. The building of the road meant that Springburn endured demolition in the late 1970s and 1980s, long after it had stopped in other areas of the city. Once the Expressway was in the Plan it became unstoppable, but delays in funding it meant that the dereliction in its proposed path lay unregenerated for over twenty-five years. With the completion of the new road and the boom in property development, much of the derelict land is now finally being built upon, with private housing.

Most of the errors in post-war housing schemes have arisen from failing to recognise people's needs except in purely spatial terms. Far less did the processes of planning involve consultation with or involvement of the people affected. Apart from the lessons we can learn from how the tenement worked, which may be of use in attempts to build communities today, the experiences told in this book raise questions about the political rights of communities whose economic base has collapsed. This is a recurring feature in an economy committed to permanent growth and consequent 'restructuring'. Clearly much more could be done to manage such changes, at a minimum providing help to maintain and develop the communal support networks which people evolve when conditions permit. This book meets at least one other basic entitlement of people in these circumstances – to have their experiences recorded.

It was in belated recognition of the positive force of a sense of belonging and of community history that a Scottish Urban Aid Grant was approved for the Springburn Museum Trust which had been established in July 1984. In May 1986 the Springburn Museum opened in the old Reading Rooms of the Springburn Public Library, one of the few buildings of old Springburn to survive. It set itself to examining and recreating a sense of continuity with the lost past, always relating it to the concerns of the present. In less than three years it had received the National Heritage Social and Industrial Museum of the Year Award 1989, and a Scottish Museum of the Year Award Special Commendation in the same year.

The museum has always made people the focus of its work, and the Springburn Oral History Project, funded in 1986 and 1987 by the Manpower Services Commission, was a natural undertaking. Young interviewers following the guidelines suggested by the Scottish Ethnological Archives in their leaflet 'A Guide to the Recording of Oral History' collected one hundred and twenty personal narratives from people born between 1900 and 1960 who had resided or still reside in Springburn. Balornock and Possilpark also figured in some of these accounts.

In recent years a new interest in oral history has begun the 'democratising' of history, which previously had been based upon the written records of the privileged classes. This valuable tool uncovers the lives of sectors of the population previously ignored – those whom Paul Thompson has dubbed 'the underclasses' of history. The application of these techniques to the lives of women and children is particularly fruitful.

The life of Springburn revolved around 'the Works', and the treasury of information in the oral history archive has been explored for material on men's experience at work, with a chapter on women in war work, in *The Springburn Experience*, by Gerard Hutchison and Mark O'Neill. As the authors recognised 'the local economy could not have functioned without the unpaid work of women, the majority of whom kept house and reared families. Those who did take up paid work, took it on in addition to these tasks.' It is this 'other side' of Springburn's community history, and of history at large, which this book attempts to record, the lives of ordinary women and children, and the life of men in the home – where men were both central and peripheral, and women were the key figures.

This volume is planned as the first of a tenement trilogy: the remaining parts will explore the lives of children, mostly outside the home; and living through the hard times – the way family and community coped with war and depression, unemployment and the darker sides of life.

The procedure for collecting this material from the few thousand pages of transcribed interviews was an arduous one. All the oral histories were sub-divided and classified into material relevant to the domestic lives of women and children, and the topics allowed to 'emerge'. The resulting subjects thus make a statement about what the informants thought was important in their daily lives.

The range of the material in the archive is naturally limited by what people were willing to talk about to their interviewers, who were generally young people whom they did not know well. This automatically excludes areas of life which people regarded as private, with both positive and negative events in their lives passed over because of their relationship to self-esteem. A book which presents aspects of the life histories of named individuals has inevitably to respect the limits they wish to set, but this does not falsify the record of what they do say. In a sense this is an extension of people's efforts to maintain some privacy in overcrowded houses and buildings, to sort out problems without the neighbours knowing. Abuse, family breakdown, alcoholism and crime all existed. But this book is about how members of a community saw themselves. It is about, in the jargon, the construction of a social consciousness, about what people think their lives meant and what they think people in the present and future should know and may indeed find useful.

Note on the transcriptions: To ease reading the dialect of the transcribed interviews has not been retained in full, as the phonetically written material, though full of flavour, is difficult unless it is the reader's own way of speaking. The degree of dialect usage varies noticeably from person to person. Some people had had elocution lessons in the past; many switch from Glaswegian to a more standardised, 'anglicised', English when talking to people they do not know intimately. Despite changes of attitude recently, many elderly people especially have an ingrained perception that dialectual speech sounds uneducated: one lady indeed requested that her narrative be re-transcribed in standard English. For those who are interested the original tapes and phonetic transcriptions are available for study in the Archives of the Springburn Museum. Difficulties with specific words might be resolved by using the short glossary at the end of the book.

Note on the old currency: For those that are too young to know or remember, before the change to the decimal system of British currency, there were twenty shillings in a pound, and twelve pennies or pence in a shilling. One shilling translated into five new pence, two shillings into ten new pence, ten shillings into fifty pence.

So for example 'one and six' was the equivalent of $7\frac{1}{2}$p; 'four and eleven' (4/11d) was a penny less than five shillings (5/-), that is a fraction under 25p; 'one pound thirteen shillings' (£1/13/- or £1 13s od) was £1.65. Of course it hardly needs saying that it was worth a great deal more in real terms. An average weekly wage for a skilled worker in the locomotive works in the 1930s was £4, and for a labourer between £2 and £3.

1

The Tenement House

'Believe it or not, eleven of us were housed in two rooms until I was twenty-one years old.'

The voice of Marion Smith, born Marion Russell in 1906, will recur, articulate and observant, throughout this book. Her description of the room-and-kitchen tenement house where she lived from 1914 until her marriage in 1927, makes a good introduction to many themes which will reappear, for the household was typical in many ways, cramped but cosy and spotlessly clean. It was a large and close-knit respectable working-class family. Marion's mother had ten children in all. Her father, a brass worker at one of the great locomotive works, was characteristic of the class of skilled worker on which Glasgow's reputation in heavy industry rested. He and Marion's mother, an intelligent woman dedicated to raising her family as well as possible on a very limited income, instilled in their children strong moral values and a sense of their own worth.

As the eldest daughter Marion soon shared with her mother the responsibility of caring for the younger children and the hard work of keeping the house shining clean. The kitchen here described was typical of countless others. It is with the clarity of a child's eye that Marion's memory recalls the fittings, furnishings and treasures of her tenement home.

All my childhood days were in Springburn. I was the first child of my father and mother, although subsequently I had eight sisters and one brother. I was born in Station Road, in a close opposite Springburn Station. It was later called Atlas Street, after the works, and now it's no more in existence.

My father was a brass moulder in the Atlas works. At my birth he was just lately out of his apprenticeship, a journeyman, about twenty-two years old. To be a tradesman was a proud thing to be in those days. He worked on the brass parts of the engines, which were sent from Springburn all over the world. When engines were going to the docks, we were kept, as children, off the streets, while these huge things were transported, with outriders and police escorts. My mother came from Dennistoun, in these days rather more posh than Springburn. She had had a very good education and played the violin. She was also a lovely singer.

Our first house was a single-end, but when another baby put in an appearance, we moved into a room and kitchen in the same close. We had been away from Springburn for a spell through Dad chasing work again, to the Carron Ironworks. The First World War had started and there was now no shortage of work, so back we came to, where else, Springburn.

I was sent on ahead with my mother to the house at 42 Gourlay Street to scrub it out while the young ones were looked after by relatives. I was eight years old and my mother made me a wee apron out of a piece of sacking. Together we scrubbed everything, floors, cupboards, pot presses, food press, bed boards. While scrubbing out one of the drawers I found a ha'penny in it. How could anyone leave a ha'penny? It was wealth. Having been given permission to keep it, I thought of what I would buy. A wee box of sherbet with a wee spoon in it? A sherbet dab? A liquorice tawse, and at the end you could eat it? A stick of ring rock, with a ring for your finger after you'd eaten the rock, with some alphabet sweeties ... play at school and have them to eat after. Some aniseed balls, they lasted ever so long. The possibilities were endless. Each of these cost a farthing, so I could have any two. I still remember it after all these years.

Our house had a coal fire in a stove, which had to be blackleaded with a paste mixed up in an old saucer, and then buffed up, and finally shone to a gleaming finish. There was a piece of velvet kept for the purpose. The steel trimmings were shined up with emery cloth. As my father was a brass moulder, the mantelpiece, above the stove, was gleaming with brass adornments, all made in the works. This was one of the perks of the trade. Everybody made things in the works. We had brass iron stands, brass candlesticks, a little brass anvil, a watch stand, which was in the form of an angel's head with outstretched wings. Your pocket watch was taken off and hung there when you went to bed, presumably watched over by the angel. Other brass items I remember – a shoehorn in the shape of a lady's leg, very daring! A small brass stool with a slot in it, which said, 'Our wee girl is no fool, she puts her pennies in the stool.' We had a solid brass poker, and on the hearth, a solid brass stool intricately patterned, about eighteen inches high. It was called a toddy stool, and was supposed to hold the kettle of hot water at your side, to make your hot toddy with whisky and sugar and lemon. This despite my dad being a teetotaller!

There was linoleum on the floor, which was polished, and a small hearth rug in front of the fireplace. The kitchen chairs were wooden, and the kitchen table was covered with a sort of oilcloth so that it would be wiped over with a damp cloth. At each corner of the table there was a cornerpiece with a horse-shoe on it bearing the words, 'Good luck.' This held the oilcloth in place and presumably blessed us with good luck whenever we sat at the table.

There was an inbuilt coal bunker and a wooden dresser alongside. Just imagine coal being tipped into a bunker in the middle of the living room! There was a black iron sink with a single brass swan-neck cold water tap. Cupboards for pots were underneath the sink, and the cupboard for food was alongside at right angles. This was always referred to as the 'press'. There was a set-in bed at right angles to the fireplace.

Above the wood dresser, opposite to the fireplace was a set of electroplated dish covers, which hung on hooks in a row. These ranged from a huge one, suitable for a baronal feast in some place like Balmoral Castle, all the way down in size to a small one. There were four of them, never, ever used. But they were a prized wedding present. The shelves above, two shelves, held a blue and white dinner service, a wedding present from the firm my mum worked for, hardly ever used, and a tea set, which my mother was so proud of; it had pansies on it, hand painted, my mother told us. This was only ever washed then put back on the shelf. Also there, in the centre, a brass jelly pan, and an orna-

6 and 7. Mrs Jeanie Thomas in the kitchen of
her room-and-kitchen house in Gourlay Street *c.* 1940.
The sink with its brass swan-neck tap is behind her.
Opposite, Mr Thomas by the range in the kitchen.

mental brass kettle. On the wall in the room there were two
great big photos, oh about eighteen inches by two feet. Lovely
portraits, one of my mother, one of my father, taken after their
wedding day.

We had gas lighting, quite new then. Inverted gas mantles,
'Veritas' make, and a glass shade. We also had a paraffin lamp.
My dad was the only one allowed to touch it, trim the wick, and
fill it. It was on a stand and quite elegant, another wedding
present. (Marion Smith)

THE ROOM AND KITCHEN

'In those days your kitchen was your sleeping area,
your eating area . . . Everything was done in the kitchen . . .

*The kitchen was the key room in these tenements – in a single-end it
was the only room. It was used for living, eating and sleeping, and is
at the centre of people's memories of family life. In tenements of this
class the rooms were not large, though ceilings were higher than in
modern houses. The lay-out was practical and remarkably consistent. Sink in the window, a 'hole-in-the-wall' bed in a recess in the
wall opposite, the fireplace with its black cooking range on one side
wall, and on the facing wall a 'fitted' coal-bunker and a cupboard
with two drawers – the 'pot-press' – beneath two high shelves, long
on top, shorter below. Also built in was a shallow shelved cupboard*

29

or 'food press'. These arrangements were characteristic of tenement kitchens of all classes of building.

People are all running today making fitted kitchens but in a sense a fitted kitchen is an old idea. It goes way back. So, you had the food press, coal bunker, and this pot press with a couple of drawers for cutlery built onto the wall, and that ran up to the wall where the sink and the window of the kitchen was. Now the sink was a cast iron sink, and it had a brass tap, which was a swan-neck shape, and you turned the tap on. The handle or knob was down at the base, the pipe came through the wooden beading of the sink, from the shutter, and the tap was fixed, and the handle for turning the tap on was just at the side, and it was a turn it on and off handle: but it was a swan-neck. It was a cast iron sink, and on top of the sink you had the wooden draining board at the side. And below the face of the sink, the sink had been boxed in, and at the right-hand side was a wee cupboard with a shelf, and all the black lead, Brasso, emery paper and all the house cleaning utensils were kept in this beside the sink. (James Baxter)

The sink arrangements are also very clear in Charlie McCaig's memories. His mention of the 'ladies only' section of the family chest of drawers underlines the lack of privacy in such crowded conditions, and the firm lines that were drawn to give a people a small amount of their own space.

My best memory of the house was the wooden shutters at the back court [the kitchen window generally looked over the back court]. On the shutters were canaries. A swan-neck tap for water. It had a tumbler stand on it and a wooden board on the sink. You put a wringer on it and that's where you did our washing ... An old country dresser and a girnal [oatmeal container]. An old wardrobe, a hole-in-the- wall [laugh] and the bed. There was the old table that was scrubbed white and the chairs. Hardbacked chairs. Then you had the horsehair chairs that were fairly stiff, they hurt your legs.

In the kitchen there were a wall clock, a mantelpiece clock, and one of they marbles. The main clock in oor hoose, he [father] got that oot of the works when he retired after forty-five years. He got that at Cowlairs. It used to hang on a spring. Oh, and I had dogs, cats ... The dog was Captain and the cat was Timothy, a tortoise-shell cat. And aye, we had a chest o' drawers. One section for the ladies and one for the boys. And ye darenae go into the ladies' section! The drawer that was private! And yours was private! (Charles McCaig)

Kitchen furniture was not generally elaborate: a scrubbed pine table, usually designed to extend, and various chairs and stools. There might be a fireside chair designated as 'father's' — a smoking chair perhaps – and a smaller chair for mother. Linoleum was the universal floor-covering, sometimes extravagantly patterned.

FLOOR COVERINGS

TEMPLETON'S AXMINSTER RUGS

5ft. 8in. × 3ft.	- 14/11
5ft. 3in. × 2ft. 8in.	12/6
4ft. 6in. × 2ft. 3in.	8/6
48in. × 22½in.	- 6/11

HEARTH RUGS—

6ft. × 3ft. 9in.	- 21/-
6ft. 6in. × 4ft. 6in.	- 37/6

PULL-OUT TABLES
EXTENDING TO 5 ft. by 3 ft.

White Top **27/6**

Polished **35/6**

ENAMEL FINISH.

9½d. 1/- 1/3
Per Square Yard.
JASPE and PARQUET SURROUNDS — BROWN, BLUE and GREEN —
18 in.—6d. Yard.   27 in.—9d. Yard.
36 in.—1/- Yard.

Smoker's Chair
REXINE or MOQUETTE
39/6

LADIES' CHAIR (Adjustable) TO MATCH
24/6

8. Furnishings from Hoey's, 'Glasgow's Largest Suburban Cash Store', 1936.

There was normally space for ornaments, and with its polished brass glinting in the firelight, the kitchen was often bright and cheerful, though some homes were certainly drably coloured and threadbare. Even when a family had other rooms to use the kitchen remained the focus of life, as in this memory of the 1920s:

Well, we stayed in the bottom flat and it was one big kitchen and a small room and then we moved from there upstairs to a two room and kitchen. We thought we were in a palace having the two rooms and a big long hall. Oh, in those days your kitchen was your sleeping area, your eating area. You had your pulleys for your washing in the winter. Everything was done in the kitchen.

Just plain wooden chairs, the old kitchen table, bright linoleum on the floor, two shelves wi' all the dishes on it . . . I think my mother was the first in the street to get rid of her shelves. There was nothing elaborate about the house, but it was always clean and tidy. (Mary Tourish)

The 'pulley' referred to was another essential fitment of the kitchen, a sort of clothes horse suspended from the ceiling by ropes and pulleys. Washing to be dried, or freshly ironed clothes to be aired were hung along its slats or ropes and then hauled up close to the ceiling where the warm air circulated. Friction between neighbours might lead to squeaky pulley 'wars' – the unoiled pulley squeaking late at night responded to by a thump on the ceiling with the end of a broom, or a bang on the floor.

In the earlier years of the period gas lighting was the norm. There was generally a gas light hanging down from the middle of the ceiling, or a mantle above the mantelpiece, and perhaps one or two paraffin lamps. The iron gas meter, perhaps providently stacked with pennies, was set at the side of the fireplace, or in the lobby, or, in the slightly better class of houses with an inside toilet, up next to the cistern. John Dowie recaptures the thrill of the change to electricity.

And it was gas we had, gas light. I can remember the first night I came home and we got the electric into the house. Don't laugh when I tell you, but a forty or sixty watt lamp. And that was your main light. A forty or a sixty, oh, we thought it was wonderful. I remember the workmen were working close by close and the first day I came home from work, oh, the stair was lit wi' ... electric light. Went in the house, oh, Blackpool illuminations! A forty watt lamp! [laugh] But still you were thrilled, you know. Oh, that was the first introduction to electricity.' (John Dowie)

For many occupants of room-and-kitchen houses the 'room' was less important as a living area than as extra sleeping accommodation. But it could also be used as a parlour for entertaining visitors round the banked-up fire, and it was here that a family's aspirations might be expressed in prestigious pieces of furniture – a bookcase

9. Robert Lister's father by the prized bookcase in the room of a tenement house in the 1930s. In the foreground is a bed-end.

10. Wilhemina Lister in the room, with its fine clock, piano, and wireless. Note the folding bed against the wall.

perhaps, or a small china cabinet – and special soft furnishings. In place of the normal small rugs there might be a 'good' Axminster carpet in rich colours covering all but the wood or lino surround (fitted carpets did not appear until after the Second World War). A mother or relative who had worked in the upholstery trade, for instance, could make floor length drapes with matching pelmet to add an effect of plush substance to the room. Sometimes a father's trade skills would be put to use making special furniture:

My father made furniture. I remember him making a lovely table, a mahogany table. And he made a chair, a big wooden chair. It's still in existence that big chair. And, at that time they were starting to make these wee radios, wireless sets, ye know, the crystal sets and he made a box thing for that. You didnae have room for a lot of big furniture in houses in these days. (Hannah Fletcher)

TREASURES AND FAMILY PHOTOGRAPHS

'I remember . . . an amber-coloured punch bowl . . .
It was really beautiful, especially when the sun struck it.
All the colours shone on it. It really was lovely.'

Special family possessions are etched indelibly on the memories of people who grew up with little material wealth, as Marion Smith's account at the beginning of this chapter showed. Again and again such things are recalled with tenderness and nostalgia. One lady spoke fondly of a seven-piece royal-blue velvet Chesterfield suite. Cathy McIlroy remembers with sighs of regret a sideboard, and an amber-coloured punch bowl from her childhood in the 1920s:

I remember she [mother] had a beautiful, what I termed a beautiful, sideboard in the room. Big bow-fronted sideboard an' glass mirrors at the back an' wee sorta shelves on it. And on the sideboard an amber-coloured punch bowl. When I think of it, it was beautiful. It would be worth a good penny now. And there was about six cups all round it, and this, a ladle inside it. But when we moved from there to Avonspark Street, it was too big a piece of furniture and it wouldn't have fitted in the new house and I don't know really what happened to it. I'm sorry now when I look back – not so much on the sideboard, when I look back on the punch bowl. It was really beautiful, especially when the sun struck it. All the colours shone on it, it really was lovely. (Cathy McIlroy)

When the basic features and fittings of tenement houses were so similar, these special pieces of furniture and ornaments helped distinguish a family home and gained great sentimental value, often as visible signs of esteem, talismans of good fortune.

My mother had a few nice things she treasured. She had a silver teapot, and a carving set in a purple velvet case ... All of these were wedding presents, never used, or hardly ever. My mother seemed to draw comfort from them ... These were her 'things', and probably helped her through the bad times and sad times. (Marion Smith)

The mantelpiece was the place for display of treasures: the presentation clock attesting valued service; the sort of brass ornaments described by Marion Smith, or the ubiquitous 'wally dugs', matching porcelain dogs sitting at each end (wally lions were a variation). The ornaments remembered by James Baxter, 'kilties' and assorted Scottish heroes, displayed a characteristic patriotism.

Now, everybody used to have ornaments, dishes and 'Wally Dugs' and sets of jugs. We had statues, kilted statues. We used to call them kilties. Statues of men in highland dress. Then we had Lord Roberts on a horse. I don't know if you've heard of him; he was a General during the Boer War, Lord Roberts. And Hector MacDonald was another famous general, he committed suicide. He was accused of being a gay type away back, and the disgrace was ruining at that time, he committed suicide in Paris, Hector MacDonald. He was a great general. In fact, they say that he won the Battle of Omdurman for Kitchener – saved Kitchener, Hector MacDonald. Anyway, there was Hector MacDonald. Then there was Flora MacDonald on a horse, a statue of Flora MacDonald on a horse that we had. (James Baxter)

Photographs were the standard wall decoration before the Second World War.

It was like the Art Galleries. The big room was like the Art Galleries. All the aunties, uncles, grannies and what have ye. (James Robertson)

11. Sam Watt's father in the uniform of the Seaforth Highlanders: he served in India during the First World War.

These 'galleries' were a visible manifestation of the importance of the extended family in this culture, and often too an expression of pride in menfolk who had fought and died for their country.

Now at that time everybody used to have portraits of their families, various members of their families, hanging on their walls. These portraits were about, well, maybe about two feet by about maybe two foot square, roughly. It was either a square or a rectangle, maybe two feet by one foot or something. But I remember, beside the iron sink, where the windows shuttered on the wall, was an uncle who had been in the Royal Engineers during the war. He had been killed. His photograph used to be on one side, and my Aunt Bella and a baby on the other side. and on the other wall, the fireside wall, facing the bunker side, was a portrait of this uncle that stayed with us in the uniform of the Cameron Highlanders. But he didn't have the kilt on. He just had the usual trousers and puttees round his legs. (James Baxter)

There were pictures of my uncles, ones who have been killed in the war. That was the First World War. (Henry Stewart)

Royalty and lesser dignitaries were other popular subjects, while pictures of faraway places were food for imagination in days before television opened up the world.

We had a photie of the minister. A photie about six foot long of the Royal Family of Great Britain. A photie of Cowlairs Works. A photie of my uncle who got killed in the war. And a photie of my father and grandfather. (Dick Johnstone)

I always remember a picture in the kitchen, because I used to say I would love to go there someday. It was a scene abroad, it was a man on the water like those gondoliers that you see in Vienna. (Isabel Miller)

After the Second World War such photographs were often put away or thrown out as old-fashioned, perhaps to be replaced with 'modern' mass-market decorations like the three famous flying ducks.

2

Beds and Baths

'When you look at it now, ye know,
you wonder how people sort of were able to fit in!
.. And the size of the room!'

The theme of family closeness comes to the fore when we consider the problems of accommodating families which were generally significantly larger than today's in one or two rooms. It was this sort of over-crowding and the attendant health risks which gave the old tenements a bad name and prompted the massive re-housing schemes after the Second World War. There was almost no private space in houses so small. The frictions this must have produced in some families do not figure in the recorded memories, which tend to speak matter-of-factly about the feats of organization involved in sleeping and keeping clean. Strict taboos protected individual privacy, and families were disciplined to live harmoniously at very close quarters to each other.

HOLE-IN-THE-WALL AND HURLY BEDS

'You know, I would have loved to have a bed of my own.'

One of the most distinctive features of the tenement house was the 'set-in', 'boxed-in' or 'hole-in-the-wall' bed in the kitchen – sold today by estate agents as a 'dining recess'. If there was another room, there was normally another recessed bed in there. In nineteenth-century tenements these were often built as bed-closets, that is, beds in large cupboards with a door; but in accordance with the recognition that ventilation was crucial to health such confined spaces were outlawed in 1900, when the Glasgow Building

Regulations Act decreed that 'No dwelling house shall contain an enclosed bed or a bed recess which is not open in front for three quarters of its length, and from floor to ceiling.' Existing tenements had to be brought in line with this ruling within five years. This is reflected in James Baxter's account:

Now at one time recessed beds were only an entrance, like a door. A lot of people knocked part of the wall down and opened them up a bit. Well, our kitchen one must have got opened at

12. Jean McFarlane sitting in front of a recessed bed *c.* 1940.

some time because as far as I remember its full length was wide open, you know ... And you had a wooden frame. It sat up about four feet high ... Bedboards were laid across this wooden frame to support a straw mattress. You had two straw mattresses, then you had a 'tick'. It was a big bolster and it was full of wool, and that was your bed base. That sat on top of your mattress. And then you put your sheet on top of that, your pillows, and then your usual bedclothes on top of that again. That's how the recess bed was made up ... You had space below the bed that you could store stuff, and that was the idea of it being so high.

Now away back, every family had what they called a 'kist'. Now, that's an old Scotch word for a chest. It was a big chest with a hinged lid on it, and there was a lock on it. You could lock it, and you kept all your linen and bed material and stuff in this big chest. Well, to have it out of the road, in our house, they put it under the bed. And in front of the bed, to hide the space underneath, you had what they called a valance curtain hung on a wire ... And you fronted that with a few chairs. When my mother was going to her bed, she had to climb into bed. Climb onto the chair and climb into bed. I suppose that's how you hear people talking about 'climbing into bed'! ... Well, I suppose it goes back to the days when the recessed beds were all high, you know. You had to climb into it, aye! (James Baxter)

The space under the bed was indeed invaluable for storage, often for another folding bed – but it could have other uses too!

My grandfather was an awfy big stern man. And whenever he came in I used to run under the bed [laugh]! I mind my mother, he had got onto my mother once. Whatever happened, my mother got a terrible row. And I ran under the bed and wouldnae come oot until he went away [laugh]! (Marion Law)

It was normally the parents who slept in the kitchen bed. A curtain across the recess might give some privacy, but the room was often shared with the youngest child or children. The arrangements described by Sam Watt were typical.

In the kitchen there was a hole-in-the-wall bed. That's where my mother and father usually slept. See in the old houses it was just a square hole in the wall. And it was what they called a bearer with wooden planks across it. And the two straw mattresses sat on top. That was their bed. Then an old iron bed at the side that folded up. The youngest in the family slept in that. In the room, that's where the brothers slept, and my oldest sister slept. We had four beds. It was a room 'n' kitchen, you know, an' the toilet outside. An' that wis your whack! (Sam Watt)

Space was always a problem, sometimes, if only temporarily, solved by moving to a bigger house.

Well, I can remember when I wasnae even at school. We were in a single-end. My father and mother were in the recess bed, my sister was in a wee bed chair, and I was in a cot. And then we really hit the big time because we got a room and kitchen. And the room and kitchen had a recess bed in the room! (Betty Knox)

Usually the growing family outstripped the available rooms and necessitated a variety of complex arrangements. Many houses must have seemed like Charlie McCaig's:

The house was so small, that [beds] was about all that was in it. Oh, it was terrible! (Charles McCaig)

When you look at it now, ye know, you wonder how people were sort of able to fit in! I mean the places were spotless, ye know, they really were. And the size of the room! We had the five of us. And it was a masterpiece of organization at night. We had folding-down beds. We had all sorts of things! (Cathy Page)

Many families had iron beds in the 'room'; but beyond that there were all kinds of bed contraptions designed to be pushed out of the way during the day. Folding beds and bed-chairs have already been mentioned; 'hurly beds' were folding beds on castors designed to slide under the set-in bed; Margaret Burniston remembers a cupboard with a fold-down bed in it that became a linen cupboard as the children grew up and left home; in Tommy Doyle's house the children had a mattress on the floor; while more than one baby slept in a chest of drawers:

The youngest one in our family always slept in the top drawer! They pulled the top drawer out and put the youngest baby into it. (John Wotherspoon)

It was common for young children to sleep together two to six in a bed, two or three at one end, and two or three at the other. An attempt was usually made to separate boys and girls into different beds, at least once they were beyond a certain age, but there was not

13. Advertisements for folding beds from Hoey's, 1936.

usually any question of separate rooms. Given the size of the house and the size of the family, the sleeping arrangements remained very similar throughout this period.

There was myself, my sister and two brothers slept in a set-in bed in the kitchen, two top, two bottom. (Cathy McIlroy)

Three sisters slept in the one bed and my brother and I in the other when we were youngsters at school ... At night we had to make down a three-quarter fold-down bed in the cloakroom. If anyone wanted into the bathroom at night, they went through the cloakroom. (James Vaughan)

I had seven sisters, four of them slept in the double bed, top to tail. The others slept in a bed in the room. I slept in a larger than normal child's cot till I was about eight years old. (Peter Russell)

Parents sometimes slept apart from each other, with children:

My mother and my two brothers slept in the room, and my father and I slept together sometimes. (John McKee)

Well, my mother slept in the kitchen with my sister, and my father and me slept with my grandfather in a big double iron bed that sat on one side of the room. I say iron bed, it had an iron spring. And the bolster sat on top of that. Then you put your bedclothes. And it had the sort of railing headboard and foot, you know, with the brass knobs. And a lot of people nowadays think this is a great thing, a luxury item, an antique, having an iron bedstead! (James Baxter)

Mary Tourish remembers being allowed to sleep with her mother when her father worked on the night shift:

Now my father was on constant night shift except on his nights off. My mother slept in the kitchen and if I mind right I used to sleep in the kitchen with her. And there was a big double bed in the room and my oldest brothers slept in the big double bed and my young brother slept in a small kind of single bed. And what happened then when my father came in [laugh] I cannae mind. They must have got a place for me somewhere. (Mary Tourish)

Illness might bring a temporary change in the sleeping arrangements so that a sick child could be near its mother.

I remember when somebody was ill in the family my mother made a bed up with four chairs. (Marion Law)

For a little extra comfort on cold nights, a stone-ware hot water bottle or a flat iron warmed by the fire and wrapped in an old pair of trousers might be popped in to take the chill off the sheets.

And finally here is another long narrative from Marion Smith which expresses the warmth of living together in conditions that would seem to most people today unbearably crowded; and her longing too for a bed of her own.

In the room was a green plush suite, two easy chairs, small chairs and a couch. There was also a set-in bed there: four children slept in it. The others slept in a 'hurly', which was a fold up bed which pushed underneath the hole-in-the-wall bed. Believe it or not, eleven of us were housed in two rooms until I was twenty-one years old.

I was always in charge of the baby before the last one. And one time, I had a new baby to sleep with me. My mother must not have been very well, I remember this. We had an iron bed, with the fancy iron work at the end of it.

I woke up with this new baby crying beside me in the night. And she had put her head through a bit of this fancy work. And of course the louder she cried, the more she was thrashing about: I couldn't get her head out. I actually managed to get her head out because I took away one of the pillows and that let her head down, and I got her head out. I remember that until this day! Oh horrors! This baby that I'm in charge of, strangling herself!

The wee ones liked to cuddle in with me, and I had an on-going story. And I used to get tired and fed up with it because some nights I didn't want to be telling stories. I wanted to go to sleep and they'd say 'Go on!' I'd say, 'Oh, I forget!' And I always remember one of them saying, 'Well I remember! You were at the wee bit where the fairy had a baby and she put it in a walnut shell for its cradle!' That's the bit that I had told them. And here I was I couldn't get out of it. They remembered the bit I was at in the story. I just went on and on and they thought it was fine. It was sort of a prelude to their going to sleep at night. I had to do this and then I'd say 'I'm too tired, I have to go to sleep', and then they'd all go to sleep.

My mother would knock through the wall between the set-in beds. And the final thing was she'd say to my father, 'Now Peter, I've done all I can. Now you'll need to go through and speak to them.' And my father was the gentlest man you'd ever know. He never lifted his hand to one of us. And he would come through ... and he had this walking stick and he would tap the bed-clothes with it and he would say 'Shh! Go to sleep now. Yer mother's gettin' on to me.' And we would then look at each other and say 'That's a shame to get him into trouble. Ooh, that's a shame.' For my mother was the one who was more nippy. But my father was always a gentle fellow.

Until I was say about fifteen or thereabouts I had never known anything else. I had no yardstick, I always had to sleep with others. Then I began to feel that I was growing up and I wanted a bed of my own. You know I would have loved to have a bed of my own.

When I started work in the assessor's office, it was nearly all men. I was put in the care of a very, very nice lady. She came from again, a more well-off strata of society than I did and she sort of took charge of me. She was a spinster, but a lovely person, and she took me under her wing as if I was her charge. And she said 'You know when you came here, Marion, you chattered on and on, and all your tales were about "our children" – what "our children" do, and "our children" do this. It put me in mind of a picture I saw, Mary Pickford in "Human Sparrows".'

This lady, Jean Jeffrey, she had heard me saying I wish I could have a bed to myself. She said 'Listen Marion, I've got a foldaway bed, that we use for an odd visitor maybe coming. If you'd like I'll send it up to you with the carrier.' So she did and I got my bed to myself. (Marion Smith)

TAKING A BATH

'Ye boiled kettles o' hot water, and ye had a good bath.'

Getting a bath or even a good wash required rather more work than it does nowadays. Though some of the slightly better room-and-kitchen houses had maybe an inside toilet, or a little scullery, few families of this class knew the luxury of running hot water or their own bathroom until they left the old tenements to be re-housed.

A couple of kettles boiled up were enough for a wash in the sink, or to fill a basin that could be carried through to the room for privacy. But for a complete bath, the fire would be poked up to a roaring flame to boil the water in the big soup pot, the kettle, and stew pans. A large zinc bath would be pulled out in front of the fire, with a piece of soap in a cup, and a flannel washcloth laid out near by, and a towel hung to warm; for a child or baby the night clothes might also be put to warm by the fender or over the oven door. While

46

an adult bathed children would be sent through to the room to protect decorum.

For Charlie McCaig working long exhausting hours as a young man in the coal pit in the early 1930s, a good meal and a hot bath, often near midnight, were his only relaxation:

When I worked in the pit ... there were no baths. Well, ye got up at five in the morning. Aboot four o'clock in the day, the gaffer [foreman] used tae say 'Yer working late!' An' ye used tae say, 'What aboot a piece?' An' ye worked tae aboot ten o'clock at night. Long, long hours, ye know.

Then ye came home. Ye missed the last bus. Ye walked fae there home. Sometimes I got home at twelve at night. And ye had a' the dirt and coal dust on ye, so ye had tae git oot the big bath and have a bath. Ye boiled kettles o' water. There were no hot water. Ye boiled kettles o' hot water and ye had a good bath, maybe no every night, 'cause ye didnae have the time. Intae the bath an' ye got washed. Ye got a full pot o' porridge, maybe three eggs, sausages, whitever was going. Ye walloped intae it. Ye went tae bed, and ye just got yir eyes shut ... 'Charlie, time for work', and ye wir awake. (Charles McCaig)

Peggy Taylor's mother had a system for bathing all the children in one evening in the communal wash-house, with father's help:

My mother used to boil up the water in the wash-house. She'd bath us one after the other and hand us to my father. She'd wrap us up in a blanket. Right, to my father! He'd run us up the stairs. And do you know what he'd say to us? I'll use his words: 'Now, that's you. You stay in that bed till I get back, or I'll skelp your arse! Well, I had a flat bum from all the skelps that I got! (Peggy Taylor)

Though people would wash at least in some fashion every day, a full-scale bath was likely to be a weekly routine.

The small children were bathed in a huge zinc bath, the very tiny ones in the sink. We older ones went to Kay Street to the Public Baths, a weekly ritual, purchasing Radox bath cubes at the wee shop in Springburn Road, so you would come out smelling of rose or lavender. (Marion Smith)

Friday night was the favourite night at the public baths, an important facility for working people. You took your clean clothes with you wrapped in a big towel, and got thoroughly cleaned up for the weekend.

Right up to I was thirty-six years old, I had to go to the public baths to get a hot bath. It was next to the steamie. They had these hot baths for the men and the women beside the pool. There were two different doors. You were segregated, naturally, an' ye had tae pay fourpence in they days for a hot bath. When ye were a bit older ye had tae graduate tae the hot baths. There wernae any privacy! And the queue was from the door of the hot baths right doon these steps, and sometimes oot intae Kay Street. Maybe twenty, thirty people in front of ye, especially, as I say, comin' up Friday night when they were coming from their work. They had tae queue up for a bath! (Betty Knox)

Having a bathroom with hot running water inside one's own house was such a novelty to Peter Russell that he remembers very well the first bath he took in his new house when the family moved to one of the new tenements in Balornock in the 1930s.

Just imagine as I have told you a two room and kitchen with cold water and just a fire to heat the house and so forth. To move up to a house like this which is classed as a four apartment house. Can you imagine the number of rooms, and the number of doors that were in it . . . ? I felt as if I was going into a mansion house! And to tell you the truth when we moved up here the first thing that I wanted and demanded of my sister . . . I wanted a bath! And I think they managed to struggle up about, oh, three or four inches of hot water, you know, to get me in. I thought this was marvellous. You could get a bath in your own house! (Peter Russell)

3

Doing the Housework

'You scrubbed everything that could be scrubbed, and polished everything that could be polished.'

It is clear from the recollections that standards of cleanliness in the tenement families represented here were generally adequate, and more often extremely high: as Marion Smith recalls, everything was kept as clean as it could be. There were exceptions of course, and some families had a reputation for being dirty. There was a social stigma attached to scruffiness, and when infectious diseases were still very dangerous, a real fear of germs. Scrupulous cleanliness made a clear social statement about respectability, and women slaved long hours to maintain it. Door brasses must be shining, the children washed and decently clothed. But small houses could be made to gleam with concerted effort, and this was a source of pride and pleasure to most women and their families.

MOTHER'S WORK

'It took ye to keep a house. After all, there
weren't any vacuum cleaners. You got down on your
knees and . . . scrubbed the floor.'

With large families and none of the labour saving devices that we take so much for granted nowadays, the upkeep of a tenement house was an unremitting labour, six or seven days a week. Even modest middle-class families had servants at this period, but in this social class it fell to the mother to maintain the family's standards. Memories of the childhood home often concentrate on children's involvement – which as we shall see was expected and necessary –

49

but behind this is the figure of the mother, constantly working. It is significant that Marion Smith who helped raise her eight younger sisters and brother, remembers her mother always at the sink up to her elbows in soap bubbles.

My mother didn't have time to get herself dressed until the older children were off to school. There was always a baby. I stood on a stool by the fire stirring the porridge. I used to amuse myself by looking at the craters form on the top. I'd think, 'Oh, there's Vesuvius, the volcano.' My mother would be combing hair, checking the younger children and nursing a baby. (Marion Smith)

With no hot running water laid on, an enormous black kettle was kept simmering over the fire. Hand washing was done daily; socks, underwear and other oddments: if there were one or two children in nappies, the work was endless ... The big wash done in the shared wash-house was a full day's work itself, as will be described later. Ironing was another time-consuming chore, done in the days before electric irons with a flat-iron heated before the fire or on the gas ring. The meticulous neatness of the end result was pleasing but also necessary with storage space at a premium.

That wash day, she started early morning. After that she'd iron the lot. She'd be up all night. And a sheet was folded into that size [about a square foot]. It was ironed perfectly. And I'll tell you she could get all that stuff in a drawer. And if you took it out and undone it, it would have been a great big pile. But you couldn't disturb her drawers. That was her way and she had her style of doing it. (James Kinnear)

Cooking pots were generally heavy and unwieldy, big enough to hold large quantities of the soup and porridge which were the mainstay of the daily meals. Washing up after a family of any size was a major chore.

It used to be a big iron pot that we used for our soup. It was the same with our stew pans. They were cast iron. They were very heavy, which was cooked on an old-fashioned range, which you used to have a black-lead every week. (Isabel Miller)

The range itself which was the focus of the kitchen, providing warmth, hot water and means of cooking, needed constant attention: its regular blacking and burnishing is frequently mentioned. It also

14. Mrs Thomas cooking at the range in her spotless
kitchen in Gourlay Street. The gas light above the mantelpiece
is visible, and the recessed bed behind.

had to be fed with coal, which was tipped into a bunker in the kitchen when it was delivered; this created layers of dust and grime which had to be constantly removed. Though coal fires were dirty they did have one housekeeping advantage:

The advantage of a coal fire was of course that you could burn other stuff besides coal in it. All the household rubbish went in the fire. It helped keep the place clean and helped keep the middens tidier. I noticed the difference actually when the coal fires were done away with. People were giving them up voluntary before modernization, but I noticed the difference in the middens. Household rubbish, food and stuff was, you know, was being thrown out, whereas before it would have been thrown on the fire and burned. (Robert Lister)

Carpets had to be taken outside to be beaten, a heavy load up and down several flights of stairs for people in the upper flats. Also

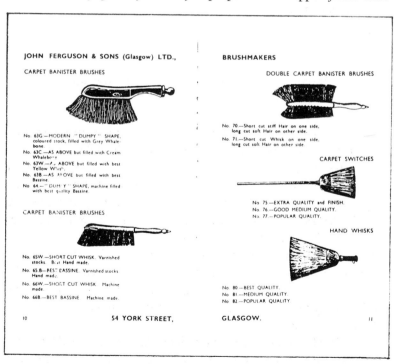

JOHN FERGUSON & SONS (Glasgow) LTD.,   BRUSHMAKERS

CARPET BANISTER BRUSHES

DOUBLE CARPET BANISTER BRUSHES

No. 63G.—MODERN "DUMPY" SHAPE, coloured stock, filled with Grey Whale-bone.
No. 63C —AS ABOVE but filled with Cream Whalebone.
No. 63W —As ABOVE but filled with best Yellow Whisk.
No. 63B.—AS ABOVE but filled with best Bassine.
No. 64.—"DUMPY" SHAPE, machine filled with best quality Bassine.

No. 70.—Short cut stiff Hair on one side, long cut soft Hair on other side.
No. 71.—Short cut Whisk on one side, long cut soft Hair on other side.

CARPET SWITCHES

No. 75.—EXTRA QUALITY and FINISH.
No. 76.—GOOD MEDIUM QUALITY.
No. 77.—POPULAR QUALITY.

CARPET BANISTER BRUSHES

HAND WHISKS

No. 65W.—SHORT CUT WHISK. Varnished stocks. Best Hand made.
No. 65.B—BEST BASSINE. Varnished stocks. Hand made.
No. 66W.—SHORT CUT WHISK. Machine made.
No. 66B.—BEST BASSINE. Machine made.

No. 80.—BEST QUALITY.
No. 81.—MEDIUM QUALITY.
No. 82.—POPULAR QUALITY.

10   54 YORK STREET,   GLASGOW.   11

15. Catalogue of specialised brushes in various qualities.

shared landings, stairs and outside toilets were scheduled to be cleaned on a rotating weekly basis.

My mother didn't work [outside the house] at all. No way. Women just didn't work in those days. It took ye to keep a house. After all, there wasn't any vacuum cleaners. Ye got down on your knees and ye brushed the floor or scrubbed the floor. The floor got scrubbed every week, and by the time ye done the brasses and scrubbed the steps and all the other things ... But my mother was quite methodical. (Margaret Burniston)

Some mothers were forced by circumstances to combine this punishing routine with working outside the house to support their family – a subject which is explored more fully in another book. Younger people might wonder how women managed to maintain such standards? The key to it was the 'method' of Margaret Burniston's mother, and the involvement of children as soon as they were old enough to do a job.

CHILDREN'S CONTRIBUTION

'My mother always taught me how to clean,
and I taught my children the same.'

The discipline of children especially in large families was essential. Marion Smith's mother depended heavily on the help of her eldest and on teaching tidy habits to the children: they were taught for instance to fold up their clothes in a certain order all ready to put on in the morning. In such families the older girls were often cast in the role of 'little mothers' to their younger siblings. All children shared in chores as part of a regular routine.

Oh, aye, we always helped, aye. We always had our job to do, ye know, everybody had their job to do. Well, I always done the stairs. An' my younger sister would do the bathroom and do the kitchen maybe, things like that. My mother would do the rest. (Mary Williamson)

On a Wednesday, it was black lead day we called that. That was the grate, the range. Chrissie and I got stuck into that, and the boys would do ordinary messages as long as it wasnae far away. They would go the messages, like of Cowlairs

Co-operative or such, you know. Just your ordinary keep the stairs clean, keep the toilet clean. And my mother did the big jobs. (Amelia Newton)

It was girls who bore the brunt of chores inside the house, while boys were typically sent out to run errands. But grown boys could be useful for heavy jobs: Charlie McCaig used Charles Atlas body-building instruction books when he was a teenager, and recounts the results of using his muscles to turn his mother's mangle (a large clothes wringer):

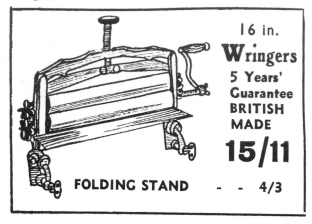

16 in.
Wringers
5 Years'
Guarantee
BRITISH
MADE
15/11
FOLDING STAND - - **4/3**

16. A wringer advertised in Hoey's Bulletin, June 1936.

Well my mother did the ironing in the house, ye know, in the kitchen. An' she used to have a big mangle that was bigger than a wringer. She used to do dungarees an' blankets and sheets an' that in this big mangle. Oh, it wis a big huge thing, ye know. An' ye used tae stand there cawing away. Aye, we used tae do an awful lot of weight-lifting an' muscle development. One time my mother says, 'Charlie, I want ye tae caw this wringer.' I says, 'All right.' So she had the stuff in it an' I tightened all the rollers. An' I was cawing away an' the roller blew off! I broke her wringer! And she says, 'Nae mair wringing for you!'

While children's contribution to the family welfare was usually a practical necessity, it is clear that it was also a very important way of passing on from one generation to the next the positive values characteristic of this social class in this period, of hard work, thoroughness and thrift.

My mother always taught me how to clean, and I taught my children the same. One of my daughters told her boss, when she said, 'You're such a good worker!' 'Well, that's the teaching I got from my mother.' My mother always said, 'If a job's worth doing then it's worth doing well.' And we always remember. (Isabel Miller)

Isabel Miller's father contributed in a different way to this training by rewarding her work with pocket-money – which was to be saved. Saving was an important cultural value in many tenement families, and in later life a girl would handle most of her husband's pay-packet.

The big kitchen dresser had all fancy plates on it and big wally dugs that had to be washed once a week, and that was my job. And my father used to give me two shillings for doing it. And I used to have to brush his shoes. And when I brushed his shoes he'd give me a wee poke of sweeties and a sixpence, and he would say, 'Now you don't spend that sixpence. You put that in your bank, that's the reason why I've gave you the wee poke of sweeties!' (Isabel Miller)

This recalls Marion Smith's father who made her a little brass stool with the engraving, 'Our wee girl is no fool, she puts her pennies in the stool.'

FRIDAY NIGHT

'Oh, Friday! It was a great night!'

Even if things got a bit out of hand during the week, there was always the Friday night cleaning, a custom which many families followed throughout this period, and one which, at first sight surprisingly, is remembered with much zest and pleasure. All members of the family were depended upon to be in and scrubbing on a Friday night. Fathers were exempt, but not boys, as Peter Russell recalls of his family's Friday night purges in the 1930s.

The general cleaning my mother would do. But come Friday night it was a cleaning night. Everything! The grate was done, the hearth was done, the table was scrubbed, the cupboards were done ... A miniature spring clean was done. Well, everybody was involved in that. And in those days the cutlery had to be cleaned – there wasn't stainless steel cutlery like what you have got just now, a wash an' that's them done. They had to be cleaned. All the knives and forks and things had to be cleaned. And, as I say, the grate was polished. So we all had our jobs to do. That was, everybody in the family got stuck in. My father didn't get involved with that! Although I was the son of the family, as a child I had a job to do. (Peter Russell)

Shining brass on the door and the mantelpiece was a symbol of family well-being; but keeping it gleaming was no easy task. It was rubbed with Brasso, which was allowed to dry to a white powder and then rubbed off and vigorously shined. Ornaments made unnecessary work, but were very important to a family's sense of identity, and are often mentioned. There would be quite a bit of brass on the average fireplace.

We had a fireplace with a big high mantelpiece. An' it had brass beading all round about it. An' a brass rod jutting out from it, an' she used to dry some clothes on that brass rod. An' there was brass boots an' brass bells, brass ornaments. An' they had all to be cleaned every Friday without fail! (Cathy McIlroy)

Along the mantelpiece you had brass tea caddies, and various wee ornaments. I remember we had a couple of small anvils that stay on either side of the light, and a couple of brass egg-cups and all that, you know. So every Friday the range was all cleaned and the steels on the range were all polished with emery, and the black body of the range was black-leaded, and all that. And the fender, if you had a fender round about the hearth, it had a steel edge that got polished as well. And sometimes the fender had a top on it, broad top, it covered a good part of the hearth. You couldn't see much of the hearth. But anyway, there was a hearth plate that you would buy in the ironmongers. It had a kind of tiled surface, decorative, painted surface . . . , setting your hearth off, you know. Now, after all the fireplace was polished and black-leaded and all that, then the brasses would get done. (James Baxter)

The Friday night routine was obviously hard work, including major jobs like carpet beating, floor scrubbing, window washing, and cleaning stairs and toilets. But a satisfaction in the thoroughness of the job, a pride in a clean house and a sense of family closeness in a special effort is repeatedly expressed.

Oh, Friday! It was a great night! It was a cleaning night. All the brasses had to be done. The table had to be scrubbed, window-sill had to be scrubbed, floor had to be scrubbed, carpets beaten, taken down to the back green. That was the kind of work that had to be done on Friday nights! Saturday, it was kind of a social day. (John Dowie)

For many families like Marion Smith's Friday night itself ended as a social occasion with a trip to the chip shop to bring back a fish supper.

Friday night we did all the housework, the house was gone over from top to bottom. You scrubbed everything that could be scrubbed and polished everything that could be polished, and then we were all exhausted and worn out.

When we finished our work, our mother used to spread the scrubbed table with clean newspaper. You didn't put down any of the table covers, that was really for company. She spread this scrubbed table with newspapers and sent to Braddock's Fish Shop in Elmbank Street for fish and chips. Nobody ever got a whole fish supper, that was unknown. But my mother carefully divided it up, giving each one a little bit of fish and some chips. We divided it all out to all the tired workers who had been scrubbing and polishing brasses. We all sat down exhausted, but enjoyed this late night treat. That was a Friday night treat. (Marion Smith)

This Friday night family routine overruled any individual wishes. As Marion Smith recalls, even at the age of twenty she was not free to abandon it.

We never got to go anywhere on a Friday. I remember once my husband, who became my husband anyway, coming up and wanting to go out with me. My mother said in an outraged voice, 'On a Friday? Oh, no Alan, she's got her work to do, you don't expect her to leave.' Picture trying that today! (Marion Smith)

Indeed it is impossible to imagine this degree of parental control today when most children have virtually no responsibility for the running of the family home. Isabel Miller was another who had to accept her mother's authority in the matter of Friday night duties, her mother relying on this rather than explanation of her poor health to extract her assistance.

I went the messages when I came in from school. Also, on a Friday night I had to do the brasses. Had to take the carpets out every Friday night. My chums would be out playing and I would say to my mum, 'How can I not get out?' She would say to me, 'You can get out if you do your work.' I didn't realize then that my mum didn't keep too well. It wasn't until later on I discovered she didn't keep good health. (Isabel Miller)

But the cleaning was done, and the house was now in readiness for Saturday and Sunday, which were the days for visiting and being visited, and cooking the special Sunday meal.

MEN'S CONTRIBUTION

'Me and my father did the housework until
he got married again.'

Men's status as head of the family and breadwinner was normally reflected in exemption from the ordinary chores of daily housework. While a woman might have needed her husband's help, she would often have refused to ask for or accept it, from pride in the fact that she 'looked after her man'. A man's assistance would normally be limited to taking children out from under the mother's feet at the weekend. Certain special 'technical' tasks like cleaning the gas mantle, again reflecting status, were kept for them – just as changing electric plugs is a father's job in many households today – as John Dowie remembers.

In the days of the gas it was a bracket that came out from the wall and you worked with a mantle, a gas mantle, ye know. And this mantle, if you just looked at it, it would break. Ma father was very unsteady in the hand because of him being what he was, you know, a locomotive driver. He used a lot of strength during the day, you know, wi' their stopping and starting it. His hand was that unsteady. Mother had always kept two, one for a spare gas mantle. 'Will you take the mantle out the box?' 'Aye, all right.' So he opened up the box and took the mantle oot, and you

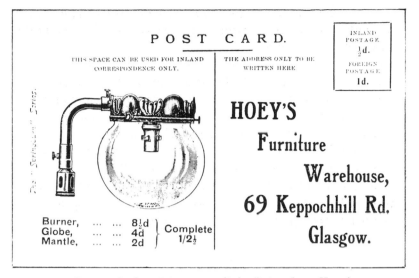

17. Postcard advertising a gas light fitting from Hoey's.

put a long needle through, you see, to catch the mantle, ... it had lugs on it ... and carry it over, ye know. [Laugh] Put it onto the gas. And first thing you did was ye turned on the gas and took the newness of the mantle, it just went up in a flame. And then you'd a globe. Every Saturday the globe was cleaned, ... the mantle was taken down. If it was quite decent it was put away and then the jets were all blown out and needles put into the jets to clean them oot. This was father's job every Saturday. Little jobs like that, you know. It was great! (John Dowie)

The cobbling of the family's boots by father or grandfather was also common throughout this period, as in these memories of the First World War and the 1930s.

Father mended the leather boots. He used to buy the leather for their boots at Tainch's Shop at the foot of Gourlay Street. That was a leather shop that used to sell leather and nails for the boots and shoes and that. Father used to steep the leather the night before in a basin of water and the next night he would get the shoes – well, it was boots in those days, boots – and he would mark off the shape of the sole and the heel and he would hammer in those nails. He used to make a good job of it too! Look what they cost now to be done! (Martha MacMillan)

Now my grandfather, when he retired from Cowlairs, well, he used to do things in the house, and he repaired all of our shoes. In these days we wore, well, boots actually, leather soled boots, and he used to do his cobbler for the family. I've still got the last that he used in the house yet, and sometimes I repair shoes myself, you know, and, well, he used to do all the cobbling and that for the family. (James Baxter)

Mrs Williamson's father also cobbled and cut hair, but when he became unemployed in the 1930s traditional roles were disrupted. This adaptation to times of social upheaval – wartime, the General Strike of 1926 and the depression of the 1930s – was not uncommon.

The likes of my father he done a lot of work in the house. Likes of cobbled all our shoes. He done things like that, ye know. Cut all oor hairs. We didn't need to go to hairdresser's. He didnae need to go the cobbler's to get our shoes mended or things like that. He did all these things, Oh, aye, he was good. My mother got a job just before the war. My father took over doing the cookin' an' that in the house. (Mary Williamson)

A family crisis of sickness or widowhood had the same effect. In 1936 at the age of fourteen John Craig lost his mother. Until his father remarried some time later, the two men took on all the tasks formerly done by the mother: in such circumstances a boy's Friday night training proved its worth.

Me and my father did the housework until he got married again. Every Friday night we steamed in and scrubbed all the floors. I took the carpets and put a big beater on them down the back. We done the washing at night-time. We'd the big boiler, so we had stacks of coal for it. You went down and lit it when you came in for your tea, by half past seven it was boiling away. By that time you put all the washing in it, and you had two sinks with hot water out of the big boiler. Then you put it out in lines round the back. Oh, there were a lot of Neds right enough, but the average people in these days all took a turn of [cleaning] the close, and you only done the landings you belonged in. That was usually done on a Friday night. (John Craig)

4

Cooking the Food

'My mother could make a meal out o' anything.
And she baked scones and things. Oh, yes, clootie
dumplin'. The smell o' clootie dumplin'!'

*Food was naturally a focus of attention in times when families grew
fast and lived on the edge of poverty; and feeding the family was a
woman's most pressing task. Though it was not easy, it is clear that
few people in this community actually went hungry, even in the lean
times. Food also has strong emotional and cultural significance, so
that it is often associated in memory with mother's love and care for
the family, comfort in hard times, special days and family traditions,
often passed from mother to daughter. People spoke a lot about food,
just as they did about the inside of their houses. Sixty, seventy and
even eighty years later, their eyes lit up at recollections of mother's
soup after school, mother's special scones, a Sunday rolled mutton
or stewed rabbit. And wafting through many memories across the
years comes the smell of the famous clootie dumpling!*

GOOD PLAIN FOOD

'I always remember there seemed to be pots of soup
and everythin' sitting at the grate.'

*From memories of childhood years before the First World War, to
the 1930s, the theme is consistent. Plain but wholesome food,
nourishing, and sustaining. John Dowie remembers from days early
in the century a well-balanced diet including plentiful rabbit and
vegetables from an allotment.*

The usual mince and potatoes, sausages and potatoes, steak. And these days rabbits were very common. Rabbit was good feed. But after the myxomatosis business came in, it put paid to the rabbits. But it wis just the general run. Plenty of vegetables, of course: ma father had an allotment so we were kept well in vegetables. (John Dowie)

From around 1930 Sam Watt remembers a typical day of meals:

Well, going to school in the morning you generally got a slice of toast, maybe went out and got some rolls, ye know, and that was it. Maybe a plate o' porridge. It varied. An' at dinnertime, well you maybe got a piece an' sausage or something like this. At night, well, your general meal was a platter of soup, ye know, a plate of soup. Maybe potatoes an' sausage or something like that. Stewed sausage or mince or dough balls or something like that. At that time this was the usual fare, ye know, and that was the run of the mill. (Sam Watt)

Even during times of unemployment ingenious mothers could include meat in the diet, as Margaret Burniston recalls of the 1920s, remembering her mother's specialities with appreciation:

Good food. We were always fed. Mother was a great cook. Well, we always got broth, and we got potatoes, we got fed, ye know. Always had butcher meat. That was something we were lucky for. Our parents would have done without to feed us. Used to make a dumpling every Thursday. This was all for economy through idle time and that. She used to make great potted meat. She was famous for all these things. (Margaret Burniston)

One source of cheap food remembered here with relish from the 1920s was the late Saturday night clearance of food which could not be kept over the weekend.

Well, one of the highlights on a Saturday night was when I was a boy, the sale of foodstuff that was not sold. Waddell's in Springburn Road, that was my favourite shop for cold meats, and they had great sausages. They used tae say, 'Waddell sausages are the best, in your belly they do the rest.' Well, it came about half past nine on a Saturday night – in these days, you hadnae any freezers or fridges. So they had tae get rid of it. Over the weekend it went bad. So, see the crowd that used to gather round about the shop, waiting to go in! You got stuff for coppers, taken away, 'cause they didnae sell it. They had tae throw it away. So we used tae get some good buys in these days. (Sam Watt)

Other families went without meat in hard times but still felt they were fed:

And in the 1930s it was porridge every morning an' soup every day, if you were lucky, if you had the money for it. But we didnae get meat every day, we definitely didnae get meat every day, ye know. And then the war started as you know in 1939; everything was rationed. But we always seemed to live all right. I mean we lived the way everybody else lived I suppose. (Mary Williamson)

Soup was the mainstay of most families, in good and bad times throughout the period. It was an economical and nourishing way of feeding a family: cheap butcher's bones or an oxtail, or the water from boiled meat (which was chopped up and served with potatoes), would make a good broth. Barley, rice or left-over porridge oats, along with dried peas or lentils, could be combined with the per-ennial potatoes, onions, carrots, turnip, parsley and leeks to make a sustaining meal. A big heavy iron soup pot was a standard item of equipment.

Well, I remember we had what ye called a Judge pot. Judge pots in those days were yon sort of iron, dark coloured iron pots, ye know. But I remember mother kept her soup pot in the bottom place in the kitchen press. It was the only place that could take it. And when she made soup there was very rarely anything left for the next day. (Martha MacMillan)

The ever-present soup pot is a strong childhood memory for many – along with the clootie dumpling. This was a boiled or steamed pudding with raisins and currants in it, wrapped in a scalded cloth: the four corners were tied together, a wooden spoon slipped under the knots, and the whole thing lowered into a pot of boiling water with a plate at the bottom of it. Sometimes it would be unwrapped when ready and 'hardened' by the fire.

I always remember there seemed to be pots of soup and everythin' sitting at the grate. The cooking equipment in those days was the big black iron pots with the handle over, and, eh, the old black iron kettle. And a wee tea pan: and good wholesome food. As I say, my mother and father were Highland and we got fed. Not fancy food but good nourishin' food: porridge, soups, stew, dumplin's, potatoes. And when I say dumplin's, I don't mean dumplin's in stew, I mean the clootie dumplin's, you know. But I never mind o' being hungry in my life when we were young.

My mother could make a meal out of anything. And she baked scones and things ... Oh, yes, clootie dumplin'. The smell o' clootie dumplin'! (Mary Tourish)

While there were certainly families who could not manage in hard times, there are many tributes to mothers who could make 'something oot o' nothing', as from this anonymous informant born at the end of the nineteenth century:

My mother wis one that could make something oot o' nothing practically. I remember goin' for the ham bones, ye know, the butcher's. And she would make a huge pot of soup. My mother wis a wonderful baker, she could make something oot o' nothing, ye know.

Food was almost always freshly cooked. Some things are remembered with particular relish. Potatoes and herring, and homemade sweets, fir instance:

Well, we ate plum pudding. Ma mother used to make totties and herring. Soor milk. Soor ploom sweeties, toffee balls. Mostly a' the women then cooked, there were hardly any tinned food. (Charles McCaig)

Porridge in the morning for breakfast was normal. But it stuck in the throat of some children:

Oh, my mother used to get mad at me because I couldnae take porridge. I was the only one. 'See you!' she says. And I used to get intae awful bother. (Marion Law)

My mother pleaded with me but I couldn't take porridge! She'd steep it overnight and then make it in the morning. But it was the right coarse porridge, you know. In those days they didn't have so much refined stuff as they have now. She couldn't afford a lot of milk so therefore it was partly water. She'd to hide the milk from ma brother because he was a great milk fiend [laugh]! (Martha MacMillan)

Families had their own odd ways in small things:

We didn't put the milk onto the porridge, we always had a cup or a little bowl at the side. And we had a spoon and we dipped. We took the porridge and dipped it into the milk, not everybody would do that, that was just our way. (Mary Williamson)

Mostly there was little room for choice or pickiness among children: you ate what was put in front of you or went hungry, as Peter Russell recalls of his love-hate relationship with mince:

About the one thing that sticks in my mind is mince was a great meal. And it was made with onions in it, that were in the mince. Unfortunately, I didn't like onions and it used to be I was told, 'Right, if you don't eat that, that's it! That's what's for your dinner, mince and onions, and if you don't like it, if you are hungry you will eat it!' (Peter Russell)

18. Kitchen wares from Hoey's, 1936.

The respect accorded to the man of the family extended to bowing to his faddiness in some families, and curtailing the range of foods accordingly:

My father had very restricted tastes. I was very grown up before I tasted a tomato, for example, because he didn't like them. We never had anything with onions in them because he didn't like them. I mean, everything was geared to suit the breadwinner, so it was very plain ... Dumpling, pots of soup, apart from that, I can't remember anything special. (Agnes McDonald)

MEALTIMES

'Any nonsense at the table and you got a crack
across your knuckles with the wooden spoon ... My father and
mother always encouraged us to talk, but the wooden spoon
was for any carry on, ye know.'

In most families, mealtimes revolved around the schedule of the breadwinner and the school children who came home for what was normally their main meal at midday. Generally, breakfast would be between seven and eight, 'dinner' between twelve and one, and 'tea', the evening meal, after five o'clock. Many people habitually lived by the 'horns', the sirens that signalled the start of work in the morning, then at noon the opening of the gates for workers who lived close enough to go home for a hot dinner, and then again the end of the day at five thirty. These mealtimes are consistent from the First World War to the late 1930s.

Well, when we were going to school we were up at half past seven or eight o'clock. An' we always had our breakfast. Then we got home from school between twelve and one and we had our lunch. And then we had to wait until half past five till my father stopped his work and we all had our tea together. (James Vaughan)

It was like a relay till we got out, breakfast, ye know. Then lunch time was usually round about midday, and we came home from school, some of us at three, some of us at four, depending on their age. But we always got something to eat, and

66

went out to play. But when my father came in we'd all to be in for our tea, which was half past five. The horn used to go at half past five. (Martha MacMillan)

Two sittings were usual in large families. Normally the older people ate first, and then the younger ones.

We ate at the kitchen table. Although, in those days, if there was any adults in the house, the adults ate first, and the children ate later. It wasn't always that everyone sat down at the same time. (Peter Russell)

Conversation was encouraged but law and order firmly maintained in Cathy McIlroy's family. As often it was the mother who wielded authority in the home.

My father and mother an' two elder brothers sat down first. And then, my young brother and the next one . . . and my young sister, four of us sat down. The second sitting. We didnae all sit together. There was two sittings. Twelve o'clock, midday, when Cowlairs stopped for the adults; half past twelve for the younger ones. And at half past five for the adults, and I would say about round about six o'clock for the younger ones.

We had a wooden table with two leafs, and my brother sat at the other end and my mother and father sat at the opposite side from my two brothers. And I may add that my mother sat with a big wooden spoon beside her. Any nonsense at the table and you got a crack across your knuckles with the wooden spoon. I always got it 'cos my brothers could throw theirselves back.

My father and mother always encouraged us to talk, but the wooden spoon was for any carry on, you know, gettin' out of hand. My mother was the boss. But my father and mother always discussed things. We were always taught to discuss things. (Cathy McIlroy)

Regular mealtimes were something that even women forced to work outside the home would strive to maintain: Catherine Richardson's father was killed in the First World War when she was a toddler, and her mother went to work in the post office.

She was never out away from her children [for long hours]. In fact, when I look at the children now, and they're eating chips for their dinner up the road! We went home for our dinner at dinner time . . . She always managed because she had duties such that she got home about nearly twelve. Then she went back about two in the afternoon. Well, she was home at teatime all right. Then she went maybe from six till eight, six till nine. We had a neighbour, we stayed in the house, but the neighbours in these days were wonderful. And next door we had a couple who had no children, and the lady was very fond of us, so she kept an eye on us. She liked doing it. (Catherine Richardson)

MOTHER'S BAKING

'Oatcakes! They were as big as a dinner plate'

Scotland has a fine tradition of baking, and this period saw the height of the great Glasgow family baking firms. Many urban housewives simply bought in their bread and cakes. But in some families baking, with its warm comforting smells, is remembered with particular fondness, often as a special mother's skill, a tradition to be passed on to her daughter.

My mother did all the baking. I think Tuesdays and Fridays were scone day, and we always had, you know, wheatmeal, syrup, soda and treacle [scones] and pancakes. And then on a Thursday she did her cakes, fruitcakes and maybe sultana cakes.

After she died, I tried to carry on more or less as she did because I had been taught from an early age. And we had a swey. Do you know what a swey is over the fire? And we hung the girdle on it. And the fire cooked it. It was an ironcast [hook] that came out from the fire and you hung your girdle on it for your pot. And you swung it back above your fire and your girdle heated that way and that was our girdle scones. (Agnes Lowther)

Many families had originally come to Glasgow, seeking work, from rural areas, and brought with them the cooking traditions of the farm, where cereals such as oats and barley were plentiful. Mrs Stronach, who learned to bake and take care of her brothers and sisters before she was nine years of age, baked like her mother for her own children in later years. She especially remembers her mother's oatcakes, baked on the farm.

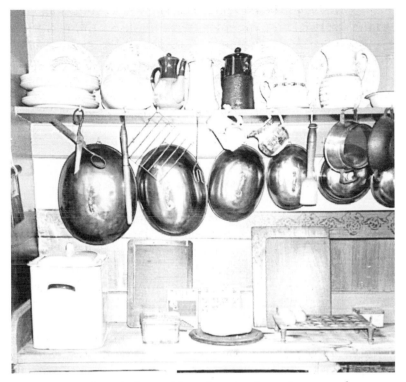

19. Kitchen shelves with various implements, some of them largely ornamental, like the handsome dish covers. Beneath the work surface were the pot press and the coal bunker.

My mother baked all these scones and bannocks. And you know what bannocks are? Oatcakes! They were as big as a big dinner plate. And she made them on a girdle on a fire outside through the wall from the house. And she could bake the bannocks on the grill, on the girdle. And then she had a toaster in front of that and she toasted them all from that and lifted them off with a spittle thing. And she would have a pile like that. And that was done every week in life. And that was to do the week. And her scones were lovely. None of us can bake like her either!

My father did his own vegetables. He had a lovely garden of fruit and everything. On the farm we got our milk and meal [oat and barley meal]. Sometimes we didn't always need flour so we got oatmeal instead. And that's how my mother could bake scones and everything. She had all the stuff there to do it with. Mostly plain food. (Jemima Stronach)

Cooking on the old black ranges in the tenements had its hazards. If it rained, bits of soot would drop down the chimney.

Aye it was an old range. And my mother used tae cook in the fire, ye know. An' she used tae pray tae God that it widnae rain because when she was cooking in this griddle maybe pancakes, and they were snow white – she'd say, 'Oh God, don't make it rain.' Because when the rain came doon, it brought bits o' soot and it dropped in the pancakes. So she was always praying. 'Don't spoil ma cooking.' It was a laugh!' (Charles McCaig)

MEN'S COOKING

'Ye felt a kind a Jessie, ye know!

Just occasionally however baking was the father's skill. Jean Parker's father, a baker by trade, did all the holiday cooking when she was growing up, and during the Second World War taught her the fine art of baking.

Oh, he loved cooking 'cause he'd been a cook in the First World War. An' ye never got near the cooker when he was in. At Christmas and New Year it was father that done all the cooking: ye weren't allowed to do any of the cooking, ye know.

I always remember the first time I made potato scones. My mum was in hospital and I thought my dad'll like them, he likes potato scones. And I had them all for him coming in. And he took one, and he said, 'What am I supposed to do with them, put them on the sole of my shoe?' It was as hard as anything! And he sat down an' showed me the proper way. He boiled potatoes and we made them properly. But he taught me quite a lot, ye know. The heat of your hand makes a better sponge and all these sorts of things. Wee sort of tips. But really, I found out now, that's the proper way! (Jean Parker)

Unless the father was in the catering or baking trade this degree of participation in home-cooking was unusual: again a woman felt pressure to 'look after her man'. But boys might do their bit in times of neccessity. Peggy Taylor's mother went to work in a munitions

*factory during the First World War as her father was ill with
tuberculosis, leaving the older boys with some cooking to do; while
Martha MacMillan's brothers helped out on wash days.*

My mother used to put the bread to rise at night, then in the
mornin' she'd put it in the oven and tell the boys to watch it and
take it out. They could do that. Oh aye, I had five brothers all
older than me. They used to make soup. Aye, they were good!
(Peggy Taylor)

Funnily enough my brothers were all fairly good cooks. They
used to watch ma mother cooking, ye know. For instance, washing day ma mother was a whole day in the wash-house. There
wasn't washing machines. My father, before he would leave for
his work, would set the fire in the wash-house. And mother was
ready to go in after she got us to school. She was in there all
morning. She would sometimes maybe keep one of the boys off
school to look after the dinner. She'd it all prepared, but they
knew what to do. And when we come in at dinner time she
closed the door of the wash-house to come up for her dinner.
She'd go back down again and she was usually finished before
ma father came from his work at teatime. (Martha MacMillan)

*Later on there are more signs of a slight role relaxation, and, just
as today, a father might do a ritual Sunday breakfast, as Peter
Russell remembers of the 1930s:*

Breakfast was a bit special. This was the thing about my
father that he always insisted that he made the Sunday breakfast! And you know, it gave ma mother a bit of a break. He got up
and made the Sunday breakfast! It was usually quite a heavy
breakfast. It was the usual full English breakfast with ham and
eggs and potato scones and sausages and whatever was going.
(Peter Russell)

*In the early 1940s there was an indication that schools realised
that there were times when young men might have to be able to fend
for themselves: James Baxter at age fourteen with some embarrassment undertook a cookery class while attending Albert Secondary
School. This was unusually progressive, and as James, well aware of
cultural norms, says, he felt 'a kind of Jessie'.*

In 1943, after the higher exams were all over, the Forestry
Commission were looking for people to help them cut the

bracken. So they started going round the school. Now, the boys that were going to go there, they were going to have to live in huts, sort of in a camp, and maybe have to cook for themselves. So the school decided to give the senior class a course in cookery.

At that time you had rationing on. You were asked to see what you could bring. The likes of maybe jam or maybe a bit of margarine or a wee bit of butter or something like that. So we got this wee sort of crash course. I remember the first thing was you made up the flour and mixed the dough up, and you rolled it and all this carry on. You felt a kind of Jessie, you know! But anyway we made a jam tart. And after you made it you got taking it home. And then we were to bring mince up and you made shepherd's pie! (James Baxter)

SUNDAYS

'I think your mother used to try to do better on a Sunday.'

Sundays were a genuine day of rest, a day for religious duties in many families, but for also visiting and almost universally for special food treats. It usually began with a special 'fried' breakfast, a nice change from the porridge and toast during the working week (even more of a change if it was cooked by father, as recorded above).

On Sunday morning breakfast comprised of fried potato scones, or soda scones and ham and eggs, maybe a sausage. We always had a fried breakfast on a Sunday which we didn't have during the week. And it was either fish and bacon or ham and egg, you know. And we always went to Sunday School, and morning church. And in the afternoon was Sunday School. And then very often we left from Sunday School to go down to my grandma's down in Townhead. (Isabel Miller)

Sometimes breakfast would be skipped for a kind of 'brunch', as Henry Stewart remembers of the lean days of the 1930s, when mince was the Sunday treat:

During the week you got up in the morning and it was a quick brekkie. A piece of toast if you were lucky, and of course you were at work all day. And the next meal was at night at five, six, or seven o'clock. But a Saturday and a Sunday was a totally different ball game, as that was your long lies. I think your mother used to try to do better on a Sunday. But my mother always used to try and keep us in our beds as long as possible on a Sunday. And for years I never understood why. And it was to save a meal, breakfast. And she was economizing in her own way. We always had a mince and loads of bread and butter for our breakfast at about twelve on a Sunday. Oh, yes, mince and tatties. And I still like them. (Henry Stewart)

For midday dinner, there was usually some kind of meat, even if it was only rabbit, as in Dorothy Wardynec's account of the 1920s:

On a Sunday. Oh, a Sunday was [laugh] that's when we had a rabbit. Invariably a rabbit on a Sunday. That wis about the only extraordinary treat we had really was a rabbit on a Sunday. A chicken or that was kept for New Year or Christmas – well no so much Christmas then, but New Year. (Dorothy Wardynec)

Others more fortunate would have a fuller meal – a roast with potatoes and fresh vegetables, perhaps fresh peas from the pod. And for a special treat a dessert: custard and fruit, or even a clootie dumpling, or a piece of cake or tea-bread. The memory of Sunday meals often seems to evoke family happiness.

Oh, Sunday we had our roast and potatoes, cream potatoes and vegetables, and she always made dumpling, and pouring custard. (Isabel Miller)

On Sunday the flank mutton made the soup, we had the flank mutton along with potatoes and veg. We cut it up It was a happy family life, very, very happy. (John McKee)

When money was scarce Sunday was the day for a treat like a thruppenny jug of ice-cream, or some buttermilk.

Another luxury we used to get on a Sunday was the sour milk. There used to be a man come round the streets wi' a big cart and he sold the sour milk. It must have been a penny a pint or something like that. And we used to go down with a big big jug to get it filled. You used to see the butter all floatin' on the top of it like. (John Wotherspoon)

Teatime might bring a bought cake as a treat, as James Vaughan remembers of a time around the First World War:

On a Sunday it was always something special at teatime. In these days ye didnae buy cakes the same as ye dae now havin'

73

tae eat them wi' breakfast, dinner and tea. That was the speciality ye had at night, on a Sunday. (James Vaughan)

When grandparents came to visit in the early 1920s, Martha MacMillan, who had several brothers, remembers twelve loaves of bread being bought for the holiday weekend:

When I got older, I were round about ten or eleven ... bread was a big item in our house. A loaf of bread vanished at a meal. And I always remember my grandma and grandpa coming to visit us on the Sunday. And it was a holiday weekend. We'd an old-fashioned dresser ... And there was the bunker and there was cupboards. The bunker was for coal underneath. And the top, of course, Mother used to lay out her bread, which she'd to cover with three tea towels. Both brown and white. Mother always bought both. I would say the likes of tea-bread and maybe currant bread something like that ye know, was extra not counting that twelve loaves. Oh yes, she had to hide them from the boys [laugh]! But she had twelve loaves, not counting fancy bread, that weekend. And on the Tuesday morning, it was a holiday Monday you see, I had to run out for a loaf of bread for the breakfast! (Martha MacMillan)

5

Entertaining and Celebrations

'People made their own amusement in those days. . .
People had more life in them in those days!'

*It is a common perception, supported by these narratives, that in
'the days before television' people had a much livelier social life than
today. These were great days for cinemas, dance-halls, cycling clubs,
camera clubs and countless other communal activities, but people
also spent a lot more time socializing in their homes. Sundays
especially were often occupied with turn-about visiting of relations
and shared meals; and the home-made entertainment of the musical
evening is particularly warmly remembered.*

QUIET EVENINGS

'We were all readers. And in the winter if we weren't
goin' out anywhere the whole family was round the fire,
everybody's nose stuck in the book.'

*In the summer a great deal of time was spent outside, out of the
confines of a crowded house, but many a winter evening was spent
quietly round the fire, reading or listening to stories. Mother's
relaxation might be mending or knitting. Children amused themselves readily with toys and indoor games of Ludo, Snakes and
Ladders, and the like, and card games were popular too.*

Well, there was a steel fender. My mum had made cushions to
put on it. And we used to sit on it. And we used to toast our
bread, and we also used to put chestnuts on it. And I used to love
when my mum would sit and read out stories to us. That was
always my memories. (Isabel Miller)

20. Eileen Lister 'reading', 1949. There were books in many tenement homes.

There were always plenty of books in the house. We were all readers. And in the winter if we weren't goin' out anywhere the whole family was round the fire, everybody's nose stuck in the book. (Mary Tourish)

Och, we had boxes, shoe boxes made into dolls' houses. We'd celluloid dolls and we dressed them up. Now we know how dangerous they were but in these days nobody thought about fire. We had plenty of games. (Margaret Suttie)

Sometimes an ambitious theatrical entertainment might be mounted using the recessed bed with its curtains for a stage. Mother might find time to share in the preparations.

In the winter we sometimes got up wee plays of our own in the room. I remember us doing Cinderella, and my mother was very good at making the costumes for us out of any old thing, bits of curtain, or outgrown velvet dresses for tunics, old hats, feathers, etcetera. At that time my Aunt Sarah and a cousin came to see us and my mother and she were the audience, and I remember my mother giving us saucers with cold sweet semolina and saying, 'Pretend it's ice cream', and we did. (Marion Smith)

People remember those evenings with nostalgia and pleasure.

Well looking back on it now, I don't think I would ever see, and for many a year I havenae seen, such a happy sort o' home. That's whit ours was. Close, warm, comfortable and cosy! (Amelia Newton)

FAMILY VISITING

'They all visited each other's houses, the families
wir all very close knit.'

Many people raised in the tenements say that families were closer in their young days. Grandparents, uncles and aunts might live just up the next close, or almost certainly within visiting range. The standing arrangements for weekend entertaining, turn and turn about, were pleasurably dependable. On the whole people seem to have enjoyed their relatives' company, and have a strong sense that the breaking down of this social contact, now that families are generally more dispersed and self-contained, is a great loss.

We had a lot of visitors. That was something that we miss, but eh, people nowadays are too tied up in this [television] and wine an' drinking an' that at night. They miss an awful lot of that [visiting]. We had an aunt an' uncle in Maryhill. They used to come over tae us one week and my mother and father would go over tae them. And we had other friends who would come up. Say about three of the seven nights of the week we had visitors in the house ... playing whist. That was a great game then whist. (James Vaughan)

Och, they all visited each other's houses, the families were all very close knit, sisters and brothers. Not like now. They used tae come, mainly on a Sunday night – they took a shot goin' tae each other's house an' playin' cards jist for ha'pennies, then aboot half past nine at night, they wid get their tea, an' went away home at half past ten. (John Craig)

Family visits sometimes had to be managed carefully where there were family tensions: Martha MacMillan remembers her mother alternating visits between her two grandmothers every second Sunday 'to keep the peace'. Henry Stewart's child's-eye view in the

1930s of class distinctions within the family is amusingly focussed on the quality of cake that came with the 'good' uncles:

Oh yes, it was always good when your uncles came up to the house. And I had a couple of 'good' uncles and a couple of 'bad' uncles. All the 'good' uncles were on my mother's side, and all the 'bad' uncles were on my old man's side. My mother's uncles were all better class. And it was good when they came because the cakes came out, and there was a good wee lay out, and you'd sit with your eye on your favourite cake and that kind of thing. And my mother did a lot of visiting in these days to see my uncles. And there was always somebody in the house. (Henry Stewart)

Marion Smith remembers typical evenings of family visiting, bringing all generations together for food, games and musical party pieces.

There was always visiting, turn-about, to aunties' houses. I always loved going to Aunt Mary. She stayed in Station Road. Food was always appreciated in those days. My Aunt Mary's party was always lovely stew and afterwards tea and dumpling or something. The aunts and uncles and grandpas sat to their meal and we were all put in a small scullery she had leading off the living room. We played Ludo or Snakes and Ladders until we were summoned for our tea.

The adults sat around and listened to Aunt Mary's gramophone. It had a big red and gold trumpet and they played Harry Lauder records. Then there were games, guessing games, Consequences and such. And there were sweets called conversation lozenges passed around with things printed on them like 'Who were you with last night?', 'Hold your hand out, naughty boy', and 'Can I see you home?'

Then plates were passed with apples and oranges carefully cut into quarters – that way each fruit did four people. The mums and dads exchanged gossip and the men spoke about the works. Some, like my mother, sang solo, or at times a duet with my grandpa, and the others joined in, if so inclined. Then all went home with an arrangement for the next meeting at whoever was having the next 'do'. It was a really close community. (Marion Smith)

MUSICAL EVENINGS AND ENTERTAINMENTS

'She had one wee song she used to sing:
"I must have a cup of tea early in the morning"
– that was her party piece!'

As Margaret Burniston says, 'People made their own amusement in those days ... People had more life in them in those days!' She spent countless evenings singing songs with family members while her mother played the piano. The effort that was put into making entertainment at home yielded enormous satisfaction and pleasure. For Mary Williamson such evenings represented the highlights of family life, though she does not pretend there were no arguments.

Oh, we've got great memories of the house, ye know, it was great. There were no television. Well, it was always a sing-song, ye know. An' your father would be playing the banjo and you'd be singing. Ma brother could play the banjo and my sister could play it. I couldnae. And we'd all be singing. No' always ... We'd always argue sometimes, fights as well, ye know. But good, quite good, ye know. (Mary Williamson)

Melodeons, a kind of accordion, were popular.

I remember my father, he was on the railway. They were all on the railway, of course. He had one or two mates. They would come and they would go for a pint. That was all they could afford. They would come back to the house, and this one had a melodeon. I always remember that. This was a great night for us. Some families had a large variety of instruments. (Douglas McMillan)

Charlie McCaig belonged to one such family, surrounded with instruments, a lot of them from the pawnshop:

Aye, in oor house there was a wall wi' a' the instruments a' tacked on tae the wall. Ye could lift any instrument practically, ye know. Mandoline, banjo, ulkalalie, guitar, any string instruments, mouth organs – mostly every instrument we had a bash at. 'Cause we were born with an instrument family, a' the family played something. A' ma sisters an' that play. It was great fun, ye know. An' ma mither used tae say, 'Stop that racket!'

But where we got most of our instruments was out the

pawnshop. Well, people put them in the pawn and no' bothering to get them. So we used tae go in. Some marvellous instruments cheap. An ye took them down, ye polished them up, put new strings on them, ye know. They were marvellous.

I had an instrument there it was aboot, oh, it must have been aboot two hundred years old. We wir at a party one night and I put it on the floor tae go tae the lavatory, an' I came back. Wee Charlie sat on it, flattened it! An' it was an heirloom, a' mother o' pearl. An' it was a beautiful mandoline, ye know. But I still play them all. (Charles McCaig)

Every boy had a mouth organ, and everyone could sing, at least after a fashion. But higher musical accomplishment was common among the people of the tenements: many children had music lessons for piano or violin.

Nan became a violinist, she was the violinist in the family ... She used to be in an orchestra. She enjoyed it. Well, she and Uncle Malcolm used to come and play the violin. Ma father was a nice singer. Ma mother wasnae a singer at all. She had one wee song she used to sing. 'I must have a cup of tea early in the morning', that was her party piece [laugh]! Our Nan had another friend that was a nice singer.

We used to have quite a sing-song on a Saturday. That was the highlight of the week and I used to bake. In these days I used to bake – I never do anything now at all. I used to bake for the crowd coming up. When they all got married and had families I maybe had about fifteen of them on a Saturday night. Ma mother used to say, 'Oh, I love to see them come, I like to see them go' [laugh]! (Marion Law)

Like Marion Law's mother, most people had a party piece, so that they were ready to do their share if called upon.

See when I was wee ma father used to sing, 'The Bonnets of Bonny Dundee'. Wait a wee minute till I tell you this wee bit. I used to think it was only my dad that knew that song and I couldnae understand how. Ma mother really knew all the wee parodies. And she used to sing, that one 'Ali bali, Ali bali bee'. And ye started to get these songs in school. I was quite put out! We always thought it was just ma mother and ma dad that knew them! (Margaret Burniston)

BIRTHDAYS

'Oh God! That was your young days, clootie dumplings
were! An odd thrupenny bit! For our birthday the big
clootie dumplin' would do, ye know.'

*In the early years of this period especially many people remember
nothing to mark their birthdays, or very little beyond a little extra
attention and a small gift.*

They weren't celebrated at all actually. I can't remember any
present being exchanged for birthdays or anything like that. It
was just a matter of, 'Happy Birthday' and nothing more than
that. (Thomas Orr)

Well, you couldnae say it was celebrations. It was just your
birthday came and your birthday went. We just got a wee bit
extra loving on that day. You know, we felt it. We would get
something. But it wasnae very much. But we thought the world
of it just the same. (Amelia Newton)

*For those who had a little more it was in those days not a cake
but a big 'clootie dumpling' which marked the occasion, containing a
hidden threepenny piece wrapped in paper. There was naturally
great excitement when the dumpling was served.*

Well, the only way we would celebrate birthdays, my mother
would make a big clootie dumplin' and put in a wee thruppenny
bit, and your pals would come in and get a slice. But I don't
remember getting presents or anything because in those days,
well, we were thrilled with the dumplin' and that was it. (Mary
Tourish)

Ah they were great days! My mother always made a
dumplin', a steamed dumplin'. A great big thing, ye know, and
that had thruppenny bits in it. It was a smashing time! (James
Vaughan)

*Sometimes there would be a present or sweets. Few children
today perhaps would be content with a dumpling and a pair of
sandshoes or school socks for their birthday!*

Well, ye got a dumpling. That was how they were celebrated.
With a thruppenny stuck through it somewhere. A big steamy
dumpling. We used to get maybe a pair of sandshoes or some-

thing, a pair of 'sannies'. Ye always got your favourite sweet. My sister was very fond of Dolly Mixtures. They wernae made up in bags then. Ye used to get them in wee quarter pounds, ye see. Ye only got two ounces. That was all ye could afford. (John McKee)

Well, birthdays in these days, birthdays wernae celebrated the way they are now. No birthday cards or anything like that. Maybe mammy made a dumpling, and maybe put a couple o' sixpences in it. And if you got a slice wi' a sixpence in it ye were lucky. That was about it. Well, a dumpling for your birthday! You maybe got a new pair of socks or something like that for school. (Sam Watt)

These memories are from the First World War and the 1920s. Later things began to be a little more sophisticated. In 1928, Catherine Richardson had a small party and a birthday cake.

When I was thirteen I got a special birthday because my sister said I was growing up now and I was to get a birthday party, and I'd get a cake. And I thought that was wonderful because I got a birthday cake with my name on it. (Catherine Richardson)

Twenty-one, the age of legal maturity, was usually marked by a big present: in 1936 Margaret Burniston got her gold watch ahead of schedule, a cause of some family friction:

My seventeenth birthday my father thought we were getting old and when you became twenty-one in my day you got a gold watch. So my father thought that he maybe wouldnae be here when I was twenty-one ... So I got my gold watch on my seventeenth birthday. And it was three pound ten shillings. And my mother fell oot wi' my dad for spending it. And I still use that watch when I'm dressed, the gold watch that I got for my seventeenth birthday. (Margaret Burniston)

CHRISTMAS

'Usually you hung up your stocking,
and you got an orange, an apple, an' tuppence in
it, and that was it!'

Christmas in Scotland before the Second World War was nothing like the important holiday and consumer season it is today. Shops did not close, and people commonly worked on Christmas Day. In some families during the lean Twenties and Thirties there were no presents for children at Christmas, just as there were none for birthdays.

Christmas time and birthdays never meant anything in these days. I don't think it meant anything anywhere for the simple reason ... there was no money, no money. The war had to come and stop before there was any money getting spent on anything. (Mary Preece)

Among most tenement families, however, it was considered a holiday for the children, and an attempt was made to celebrate it with a small present in the top of a stocking hung by the fire or at the end of the bed at night. The stocking might be filled almost to the top with cinders, with a little toy or an apple or orange perched on the top.

Christmas when we were young, ye hung yir stocking up and ye says, 'Oh, I hope I get something good!' Ye wakened in the morning, this is true, it wis filled wi' ashes from the fire, an' maybe an apple or an orange if ye were lucky, on top of the ashes. So when you got up and felt the stockings, oh ye thought it wis full of stuff an' it wis all cinders, just all ashes. It wasnae always like that. But most o' the time! (Charles McCaig)

Yes, we used to get Fry's Cream in our stocking at Christmas [laugh]! That's what ye got. Ye didnae get a big teddy bear or dolls or anything. Ye got a wee horse and a wee tin soldier and your Fry's Cream chocolate! (John McKee)

A typical toy for a child was a torch or a mouth organ. Cathy McIlroy's brother was so excited to have a torch that he used up the battery in one day.

I remember ma brother, he was a milk-boy, ye know, they had their ane barra ... an' he got a torch for his Christmas ... and it was snowin' that particular Christmas and it was dark in the mornin' ... He was up and doon a' the closes with that torch! And the battery was done before the night-time. (Cathy McIlroy)

There was a clear hierarchy of toys, as Sam Watt remembers, from mouth organs up to 'middle class' toys like scooters.

The 'top' presents at these times, the actual 'proper' toys was, the clockwork engine. A train set you wind it up, and roon and roon and roon. That was it! That was a great thing – a clockwork engine! Then you also had dolls for the kids, and a scooter. That was the kind o' top toy. You had tae be kind o' middle class tae buy a scooter. The usual toy was a metal mouth organ. The wee mouth organ cost you sixpence or ninepence. The mouth harmonium they called it at that time, ye know. Then you usually hung up your stocking, and you got a orange, an apple, an' tuppence in it, and that was it! (Sam Watt)

'Big toys' like scooters were so rare among tenement families that children would offer the owner a sweet to have a turn with one.

21. James Baxter and brother, proud owners of a 'big' toy in the early 1930s.

My husband Bill said his childhood at Christmas was a torch, or a whip and a peerie. If any kids where he lived came out with a tricycle or a scooter, ye'd say, 'I'll give ye a sweetie for a shot on yer scooter.' And they wir the big shots because they had the big toys that we were all wantin' a shot of! But that didnae mean to say we wernae happy in our own wee life! (Betty Knox)

Surprises were difficult to arrange in such cramped house, as Henry Stewart recalls:

Well, there was a lot of memories, but I think the best was always on Christmas morning when you woke up, and in a house that small, it was difficult to hide anything, and my sister usually briefed us on what we were getting. And under the bed was always a stonewall certainty as a hiding place, as space was so tight. And you would lie and imagine that you heard Santa Claus and then straight up as early as you woke up [laugh]! And one year my mother and father found out and gave her laldy! But I never tasted turkey until I was married, no! Usually the very best you would get was a steak pie, which you also got at funerals. (Henry Stewart)

Turkeys were too much of a luxury for most tenement families, though some could afford a celebratory bird – a goose perhaps.

There was six of us in the family, an' I mind my old man saying or mother telling me that Christmas time, my old man gave her maybe two pounds. And that got Christmas for everybody in the house. Well you never got any turkeys or chickens or nothing. Mother maybe used to get a wee bit o' meat or something an' cook and that was it. (Sam Watt)

Well Christmas, we always looked forward to Christmas, and we maybe got a goose. My mother liked a goose, you know, but she couldn't get it in the oven; it was a woman up the stair, she had a bigger oven and this was a great event, she had to cook the goose. So that was that ... and there were always somethin' [in the stocking]. An apple or an orange, that kind of thing. (Tommy Doyle)

Agnes Lowther, whose father was a gardener for one of the 'big houses' in the well-to-do Balgray Hill area of Springburn, remembers an unusual table decoration on Christmas Day:

My father had raspberries on the next year's wood, it was

such a mild winter. And for the Christmas dinner decoration for the table he had two sprays of raspberries. I remember [the story] actually went into the Springburn News. (Agnes Lowther)

Christmas trees were rare in early days but an expected centre-piece later. During the Second World War, Isabel Miller made her own.

I went round the back and I cut a hedgling and built up a tree myself and decorated it myself before I would let them come down and not see a Christmas tree! (Isabel Miller)

James Vaughan was one of the fortunate children who had special outings at Christmas: he remembers being taken to the city centre of Glasgow to see the big shops and have tea in a tea room. Anderson's Polytechnic was a popular department store on Argyle Street, now rebuilt; Wylie Hills had a long-standing reputation for its toy-department.

There was always a time at Christmas we were taken into the town on Saturdays and we went intae the shops. Up there in Wylie Hills ye had all the big fancy Christmas places and big Christmas trees and things like that. And see yer Lewis's, before it was Lewis's it was Anderson's Polytechnic. We were taken into a tea room and we had a cup of tea and pie. I'm talking about times before the First World War.

I got a Meccano set for my Christmas. The next Christmas I got a 1A, 2A, 3A, and that made it intae the bigger set and it finished up an' got the whole gamut of the entire parts! Now I used to get into the room and play about in there building models. I would get more enjoyment out of that than I could doing other things! (James Vaughan)

Santa Claus appeared at the Co-operative Hall in Springburn in the Twenties and the Thirties:

The main hall was done up with pathways and that, with all the different toys. And I always mind they had a big chute, and a Santa Claus at the bottom. And you paid your sixpence and this guy, he spoke into something and he pulled a lever and your present came out doon this chute. (Sam Watt)

22. Jennifer Halley and her brother with Santa Claus
at Lewis's in 1948.

NEW YEAR

'All the men got drunk. We were all laughing
an' all the neighbours came in, an' we hid
a sing-song. It wis great.'

*New Year's Day was always the big holiday for adults in Scotland,
and has only recently been approached by Christmas in family
importance. Everyone had a holiday, and it was the occasion for the
best meal of the year, and a lot of neighbourly partying.*

But the big meal, the big celebration dinner, you know, the
goose or the turkey or whatever it was in these days, that was
reserved for the New Year. New Year was more important to my
granny than Christmas ever was. (Robert Lister)

*Drink seemed essential, but it was expensive. Sam Watt's father
saved in a club a shilling or two a week for this New Year's bottle –
whisky was 12/6d a bottle, a 'screw-top' bottle of beer ninepence.
'Changed days!'*

New Year! Well ... there were a awfy lot of Andy Caps going
aboot. My old man liked a right good drink, him an ex-army man
an' everything. So my old man had a bottle at New Year and he
had six McEwan's screw-tops. That was the run of the day then.
My mother had a big ashet and that was all cooked up with stew.
And we took it up to Torrance's the bakers – was up in Hillkirk
Street, an old baker's – and they put a crust on it for pastry, this
big steak pie. (Sam Watt)

*At the heart of New Year tradition was the custom of 'first-
footing', visiting neighbours, friends and relations to bring in the
New Year.*

As a matter of fact up till a couple of years ago I have
first-footed my neighbours for thirty or forty years, and always
taken coal in. And I used to have some lumps of coal in my
garden, little bits. But I'm afraid they've gone now. So we might
do with a potato now. Oh, yes, that's another old Glasgow
custom: a potato, and you put it away carefully. You don't
throw it in with the rest of them, to cook or anything. It gets put
away in a dark cupboard an' if it sprouts, long, long tendrils the
better your luck will be for that year! (Robert Lister)

23. Robert Lister welcoming 1934 in traditional manner: photographed by his father, R. H. Lister, a member of the Eclipse Camera Club.

James Kinnear's account shows that for men whisky was essential to first-footing, and explains how despite all the fun the system was carefully regulated by give and take.

The principal thing ye had tae get was a bottle of whisky for first-footing. You had to save up for it: it wasn't easy to afford. You saved for it. So ye had a wee half bottle. So before ye went tae your eventual party, ye went tae friends. And ye went in there with yer bottle. And ye had to be dark-haired. If ye weren't dark-haired, ye had to carry a piece of coal. If ye were light-haired, if they hadnae been first-footed before, they probably wouldnae let ye in. They'd tell ye to go back, 'yer bad luck!'

But if ye went in there, the first thing they did was offer you a drink, a shot of whisky like. So you drank the whisky and they wished you all the best, then immediately after, you gave them a shot of your bottle. On the table they had the shortbread and the currant cake, the black bun, and they'd offer ye a piece of that. Ye stayed and spoke tae them for a wee while like, and then ye left and ye had tae go see another one. Sometimes in my case, I'd have tae bring in the New Year at my own house, and at my mother's and my sister's. But I had to visit people in my close, three people for about five or ten minutes, and I had some friends. It wasn't easy to get there [laugh]!

Ye started wi' a full bottle of whisky. By the time ye got tae where ye were going, sometimes half of yer bottle was gone. So that meant that you'd drank half a bottle of whisky, because they'd given you a quarter of it back. So eventually you get to your destination, ye do the same thing with your host. You give him a shot and wish him a happy New Year. Whatever's left in the bottle ye kept it, for this was for the party. Ye sat down and ye drank a glass of beer and a shot of whisky; ye washed your whisky down with this beer.

A continuous round of singing, dancing, eating, and general sociability was the pattern of the New Year holiday. It was amazing how many people could be packed into a small room.

Now most places there wasn't a big carpet, ye just took away the wee carpets, and ye were all squashed in and dancing like the Gay Gordons, or the quick-step, fox-trot, waltzes. Just in a wee room, all right together … The table was put in the other room and it was completely bare. So it was big enough to do the dancing and the games. Oh you would have thirty or forty people in a wee room playing a reel. It was really good.

At some point there would be a break for food – mince pies, or steak pie and apple tart perhaps, then more dancing and games, on into the small hours.

The fun they had there was the dancing. They used tae play the records before and after the New Year. You danced in the room, and then they would have a singing game – spin the bottle and you had to sing a song or do a forfeit … You used to do all sorts of stupid things. You had to stand in the front on a seat and shout out at the top of your voice 'I'm my mother's big pet'. Out on the main street! As long as they had a window facing it and they could see you. This was the sort of forfeit. Oh they had all sorts of forfeits.

Forfeits and games of 'Cushiony', 'Postman's Knock' and so on often revolved around sexual innuendo and kissing any women present. In this way New Year fun allowed an annual suspension of normal codes of behaviour, though the limits were strictly drawn and observed.

There was people of all ages playing, from little kids that size tae grandpas … It could be a wee, wee girl or a granny … And then there was another game, ye'd get a bag and put a man's thing in the bag like a watch. And somebody would turn his back in case he knew whose it was and somebody else would take something out of the bag and say 'What's this man got to do?' And he'd say … do all sorts of things and suggestive things. Like they might say 'Take her through to the room and show her the size of it.' And the young boy's all embarrassed. But one of the older men would get ahold of him and say 'Ye take her out tae the room and say "That room is twelve feet this way, and it's ten feet that way and it's eight feet high." '[laugh]!

As I say, it was all fun. There was no people taking advantage of anybody. Say there's a guy dancing with a younger woman and he was touching her places he shouldn't of touched her. Ye'd only need to go over and say 'Watch old so-and-so, his hands are roamin' ', and all that. And any person doing these things, he was beat up and thrown out. There was no one doing anything real bad. In most cases you never seen or heard of anything like that. (James Kinnear)

At New Year, aw, it was a laugh. An' there were nae fighting. Everybody was that sociable, an' really loving people in them days, ye know. There were nae badness. (Charles McCaig)

So New Year was a great binge of friendliness and high spirits, an overt celebration of neighbourly closeness.

And this went on from eight o'clock at night till four in the morning. And that was just the start of your New Year. You'd have the party one night, the people downstairs or next door held the party the next night, it was the same thing. Ye'd have it for four days. Now in between times, ye went tae bed, ye slept maybe for three or four hours and get up. The first thing you do, ye get a shot. And ye go and visit some people and maybe first-foot and maybe ye talk to them, or they would come and visit like. And then at night time ye'd start all over again. And at the end of three days, ye were all finished up. As I say, it was all fun.

Nobody drove a car in those days, and a taxi was too much ... so if people came from far away, and the tramcar was finished by twelve or two o'clock in the morning, if ye couldnae put them up Mrs So-and-So downstairs would say 'Don't worry, I've got room downstairs.' Just lie on the coats, or six to a bed. It was very friendly up oor close. This was your home, this was your life, up the stairs. (James Kinnear)

6

Up Oor Close

'It was very friendly, up oor close. This was
your home, this was your life, up the stairs. This
was where you did your courtin' too.'

*Up oor close: the phrase epitomises the sense of belonging, the
sociability and neighbourliness so keenly missed by people who
remember the old tenements and the old times. The families sharing
a close, or common entry way — leading to the back-close (the
passage out to the shared back court) and the stairs to the houses on
the upper floors — formed a mini-community. It was a minority of
houses at this period which had inside toilets, so toilets too, on the
landing, or between landings on the stairs, were shared with other
families. The stairs and close were busy with people passing in and
out. As James Kinnear's words show, the close was the centre of life,
and families were bonded by a friendliness which was a necessary
lubricant of crowded living conditions.*

DOORS AND STAIRS

'The neighbours up oor close were
great neighbours! The stairs were clean, the toilets
were clean, the brasses shinin'!'

*Just as the routines of cleaning inside the house held families tog-
ether, so the strict rotas required for cleaning the toilets, landings
and stairs enforced the togetherness of the close. The degree of
cohesiveness between the neighbours certainly varied from close to
close. But generally, closes had 'reputations', and there was consid-
erable pressure to keep up standards and appearances.*

The front door made a social statement. The brasses diligently cleaned on the Friday and rubbed up during the week told the world that here was a woman who was 'house proud'. A step scrubbed and whitened with pipe clay, free of scuff marks, implied that the inside of the house was scrubbed just as clean. This may not always have been true, of course. But a whole tale was told with the withering remark, 'Oh, see her! Her step is as black as the Ace of Spades, and she never does her brasses!' Thus standards of cleanliness, orderliness, and respectability were very effectively proclaimed and maintained by the doors and stairs of a close.

If someone didn't keep the door clean, that was the slum department! They would talk about her. Sometimes they'd shame her into it, to do it properly. They'd sit and talk, and get into little groups, and they'd yak and point like that, and the person would begin to realise 'Well, maybe I should do it.' They might come face to face and tell her 'Yer place looks terrible and yer giein' us a showin' up.' But that was the exception. People really kept the place up. And it was very, very friendly, very friendly. (Margaret Peterson)

There was a good deal of brass on most people's doors, just as there was inside the house.

All the doors were brass name-plates, handles and letter-boxes. That thing had to be immaculate. If there were any fingerprints on the letter-box it was polished. And the door was polished with a stain or washed. (Margaret Peterson)

Everybody had a big brass name-plate, and you had a brass doorbell about eye level. It was a push and pull bell. There were no electric or battery or winding-up bells then. It was just a push-pull bell. There was a rod inside the house and a round spring with a bell hanging from it. This wire came down and I think there was a return spring, you know. When you pulled the bell it sprung back itself.

Now some people had letter boxes, and other people didn't bother fitting them because, the factors didn't provide a letter box. A lot of people thought, well, the postman can chap the door, which he used to do! My grandfather never had a letter box. He got very few letters. Any that did come, or voting papers, the postman just knocked the door and handed them in. If you weren't in he would give it to your neighbour and they would hand it to you.

... The brass ornaments, the name plate and the facing at the door mantle were all polished. We had a wooden step on the landing outside the door ... Now the purpose of the step, I think, was to keep the draught from coming in the bottom of the door, and also to stop the door getting dirtied when people were pipe claying, because it was maybe about an inch high or something like that. Now, it was a hard white wood and it always got scrubbed to get clean. And after they'd been washed they put a newspaper over it till it dried properly, you see. Same thing happened when the top landings of the stairs got washed. Because they might be slippy with being damp ... So people put down newspapers, especially in the lobby. It was a wooden lobby, it was always wood, and it had to be scrubbed too, it was kept scrubbed.

Now, outside a lot of people's doors they used to keep a straw, well, a rough mat, doormat as it was called, for cleaning your feet before going in the house. But our house, being right on the top of the stairs, this was rather dangerous, keeping a mat. Somebody coming down the stair could step on it, fly down the stair, so my grandmother or that never bothered putting the mat outside the house. It was always kept in behind the kitchen, before you went into the kitchen door. You cleaned your feet there. (James Baxter)

Scrubbing the landing outside the front doors, and down the stairs to the next landing, was a task done on a rota by neighbours sharing a landing. A scrubbing brush and a cloth – perhaps a worn semmit (undershirt) or an old towel – a bucket of soapy water, and sometimes another one of clean water for rinsing were the equipment, with something to kneel on, as the stone stairs were hard, and very cold. Finishing touches included polishing the banisters and shining the brass knobs put near the bottom to discourage children from sliding down – which they never did! – and perhaps the flourish of a pipe-clayed design down the side of the stairs.

Mother used to use [pipe clay] for whitening the stairs of the tenements. Sometimes they did down the sides [of the stairs], sometimes they did it right across the whole lot. It brightened up the place, you know. After they'd done it they'd put a design down the sides, you know. They'd either put a big thick band down, or squiggles all the way down. It all depends which type of close you stayed in. (Andrew Stuart)

SHARING TOILETS

'We all shared the one toilet. But I will say
this, the toilet was spotless . . . It definitely was
clean for an outside toilet.'

In closes where the toilet was on the stair, two to five families might share it – leading to inevitable queues.

We had one toilet on the stairheid. Two families. There was about eight of us, eight next door, ye know. And ye had to stand waiting your turn whether ye wanted a turn or not. Ye had to stand there and wait, ye know, it was comical. (Charles McCaig)

Sometimes it wasn't so comical, and a private toilet is remembered here with feeling as the greatest benefit of leaving the tenements to be re-housed.

We stayed on a five door landin', so that there could be anythin' up to thirty-five, forty people usin' that toilet, so you were aye queued up for it, so if you were caught short – and in these days the lack of food and everythin' it affected your bowels, you know, diarrhoea and such like – you had a terrible job, you know, if you were caught short, somebody in the toilet and you were waiting to get in. That was a thing, when you flitted out of that into a house wi' a toilet, it was the greatest thing that happened in my life . . . It was a bigger change even than getting the extra space, just to get the toilet to be used whenever you wanted it, you know. (John Wotherspoon)

The state of the shared toilet was the key to a close's reputation: a dirty toilet was a great source of embarrassment and made a statement about the standards of the close; and a clean toilet symbolized a 'good' close and good neighbours. There is consistent emphasis on the high standards generally maintained.

Well, believe me when I tell you they were spotless clean. Because all the neighbours took their turn of cleaning it out. It was really kept clean. (John Dowie)

We all [about twenty adults and children] shared the one toilet. But, I will say this, the toilet was spotless. It was white-washed regularly, plus it was disinfected. Of course, it wasn't disinfectant as ye use in present day. It was bleach. It definitely was clean for an outside toilet ... After doing the wash in the back court I used tae take the water, the boilin' water out the boiler, an' I used tae come up and do the stairs wi' the boilin' water, and flush down the toilets an' that! (Agnes Muirhead)

Peggy Taylor recalls that the discomfort and inconvenience of having to go outside was sometimes exacerbated by boys who did not share this sense of responsibility for the common good!

Although the chamber pot was kept under the bed for the wee ones, we bigger ones went outside our landing. There was two toilets. Put on your coat, it was outside your door, and you saved all that [chamber pot] mess. But the boys, they were bad. They put tins down it and they choked it. And we had to go and hunt for another toilet to get into. They were soup tins. They thought it was funny. We didnae think it was funny! (Peggy Taylor)

But for some people the outside toilets were a source of humour: Marion Law had an elderly uncle renowned for his stories about animals living in the shared back-court toilets:

The lavatories were out in the back court. When we were very young he would say, 'I'll go out and feed my elephants.' He was kidding on there were elephants [laugh]. He used to look through the keyhole you see. He used to say, 'See them, they're gettin' their ham and eggs.' Oh, he was really funny, Uncle Jimmy. And I believed that for an awful long time ... He was over ninety! But we were supposed to see the elephants through the keyhole. He never opened the door, ye know. What an imagination we must have had in these days! (Marion Law)

Even the memory of the hardship of freezing winter and burst pipes evokes happy days for some.

In the winter-time when the pipes burst, all you'd get was water running down the stairs. The toilet on the top flat had gone wonky. Burst pipe! All the water would come doon. Oh, we hadnae much money but we were happy. Happier noo than what they are wi' all their money [laugh]! (Martha MacMillan)

NEIGHBOURLINESS AND THE OPEN DOOR

'I've seen every door being left opened on the
landing. Every door for three stairs up, every door left
open. Oh, no fear of burglars!'

*There is repeated and very warm emphasis on the friendliness of
neighbours, who saw each other constantly in the daily to-ing and
fro-ing of close life. One or two women are remembered as the kind
who were proprietorial about their back courts and would chase
away children from another close. But these were the exceptions.*

And people were so friendly, the neighbours. Ye might have
one neighbour who wasn't very friendly. But as ye came down
the stairs, 'Hello Mrs Storey', 'Hello Mrs': have a wee blether on
the landin'. (Margaret Peterson)

*The tenement house door in these days often stood open. This is
recalled as another stark difference from today, with several eloquent
testimonies to the general kindness and honesty of neighbours.*

24. 'Close chums', 1934. Photographers toured the closes taking
these group pictures to sell to children's parents.

An' then another great thing in these days was doors. Ye could leave yer doors opened. I've seen every door being left opened on the landing. Every door, for three stairs up, every door left open. Oh, no fear of burglars or anything at all. But oh, as I keep sayin' tae ye, Springburn at that time really was an entirely different place to what it is today. (John Dowie)

There was a great homely feeling. If you lived in that block of red sandstone tenements across there, you never locked your door. I'm not saying that neighbours trailed in and out your house all day. But ye never locked your door. And if ye had children, they didn't play oot in the street. They played in the back court. And they came up and the door would be open, ye know, it would just be open. It would never be locked. (Mary Preece)

The open door was a manifestation of the neighbourly helpfulness and generosity which was indeed essential to survival – which provided a jug of soup for a family hit by unemployment, or parcelled out 'close' children to be cared for while a mother was in hospital.

25. 'Close chums', 1936, in the back court of 68 Gourlay Street on the corner of Crichton Street.

I mean you always found somebody to help you. That was one thing about the place. There was always somebody to help you. Because your neighbours used to come in, and you could leave your door open. It's just a wee daft check key. And your neighbours could go in. If they wanted a wee bit butter they came in an' took a wee bit butter, an' if you needed sugar they gave you sugar. It was great, it was fantastic! It was more like the one big, big family. There was no quarrels. There was no bitterness. There was nothing.

If the door was locked, the key was often in the door. The key in the door said plainly, 'We're out. But you can come in.' Turning the key placed an obligation of honour upon the person entering to do no harm. A neighbour could come in for a cup of sugar and leave a note, or mention it later. A visiting relative or friend could come in and have a cup of tea and wait for someone to come home. And if the key wasn't in the door, it was most likely suspended on a string behind the letter box, easily retrieved. James Baxter recalls the honesty of neighbours in the 1930s, with an interesting allusion to the street gangs of the period who were seen as the guardians of young and old.

Showing you how reliable people were in these days. Being trustworthy, you could leave your key in your keyhole in the outside door and go away out your messages, go wherever you liked. And your key was there for any of the family that wanted to open it! Another way of doing things. Instead of actually leaving it in the keyhole, people who had a letter box would tie the key onto a bit of string, put the string onto the outside door handle and then drop the key into the letter box, so it hung inside the door. So you used to see bits of string sticking out of letter boxes. This was people's keys.

There was very few house-breakings going on. Generally people who were working class never stole from each other. The same situation, nobody had anything worth stealing. Just family things. Although maybe the ornaments, they could have been pawned to get money. But nobody thought of sneaking in the way they do today. At that time, too, if anybody attacked an old person or a kid, the gangs at the street, to a boy, the big chaps, you know, the corner fellows, got a hold of them. They'd give them a bloody good hammering, you know. So old people could walk the streets without being mugged or anything. Safe. But the tough men, although they fought among themselves, they respected age. (James Baxter)

For Marion Law the helpfulness and honesty of neighbours is what made life better in pre-war days, despite material poverty.

It was a far better life in those days. Oh, it was good. Naebody had a lock on their doors in they days, ye know. Just an auld check key fitted everybody's door. There were no burglaries or thieves. Oh, they were all very nice people. Oh, they were good. They were good neighbours. We all helped each other. Well, I mean, you could leave a check key in the door . . . you could shut your door and leave. Nobody would have bothered. Nowadays things are entirely different. It was a far better life in those days, and mind, ye had nothing. But it took every penny to keep seven of us because ye hadnae anything else and sometimes it wasnae so good, ye know.

CLOSE VISITORS

'Then he would run in and he would shout, 'Coal! Coal!' at the bottom of the stair, loud.

Closes were busy places, with the coming and going of families, friends and relations, and the regular visits of familiar figures like the gas meter man – who came in those days not to read a meter, but to empty it – and the rag woman.

The other highlight was when the man came to empty the gas meter. It was a 'penny in the slot' and he left a neat pile of pennies as your rebate on the dresser. Many a crisis was averted by the timely appearance of the 'Meter Man'. Indeed, the news ran round the street like wildfire and nobody would risk going out in case they missed him. (Marion Smith)

The rag woman used tae come up regularly. Ye kept all the old togs below the bed, maybe in an old bath. Now when the rag woman came up and ye gave her the clothes, she had tae give ye something. Ye see a lot of them were gypsies. They had tae give ye something or it would bring bad luck or break a friendship. Sometimes it was a cup and saucer or a ha'penny. Sometimes it was only a kiss and a cuddle. And mind you, sometimes they hadnae washed in a long time! But ye took the kiss anyway. And sometimes ye had her in and gave her a cup of tea. (Peggy Taylor)

The coalman and the chimney sweep were a source of abiding interest to children:

We used to feel sorry for the coalmen having to carry coal up to the top flat. Right up till even the end of the war, some of the coalmen still had a horse and cart. One of local coalmen's name was Georgie Braddery, and he was a wee bloke. He was just about my height, about five foot five or thereabouts. He was quite a tough wee guy. The coalmen wore a leather shield on their back for protection, and it was strapped to them. He carried a bag for his money over his shoulder, the strap over his shoulder, and when he was carrying the coal the bag was round at the front of him. He would back himself onto the lorry and get a hold of the bag and then the top end of it, if he didn't have a mate to heave it onto him, he managed to do it himself. Normally they had someone with them that jumped up onto the lorry and would lift the bag onto his back, his shoulders. Then he would run in and he would shout, 'Coal! Coal!' at the bottom of

---

---

26. Chesney's advertising in the *Springburn Advertiser*, 1925.

the stair, loud. And of course everybody that was expecting coal would have their door open and their bunker lid open. He could just run in and dump it, you know. In the wet weather it was heavier, I mean it was a hundredweight of coal he was carrying, and in the wet weather it was actually heavier. So I mean they really worked for their money.

I tell you one of the things I particularly remember in the street were the coalmen coming round. Horse-pulled, yes, a horse-drawn lorry. We usually got Chesney's coal. My mother fell out with the Co-operative coalman because nobody was going to tell her that that was two-and-thruppenny coal when it was really only one-and-nine. Because she didn't have a husband that was a miner for nothing! She knew the difference between the good coal and the not so good coal! So we usually got our coal from Chesney's. But it was a go-cart came round, somebody yelling, 'Coal'.

There was Reynolds the sweep who used to sweep the chimneys ... and that was quite a thing, watching the sweep, you know. He would come along and he would come into the house ... open up the flues on the range. He would pin up a big bag over the fireplace to cover it, to keep any dust falling. Then he would go away up to the top flat. From that, went up through the skylight and got into the loft and got out onto the roof. And then he would go along to the chimney, and he would shout down maybe, he would make a noise. And you had to go out maybe and wave, or shout up that he was over the right chimney or something like that. Then he could drop his brush. It was a sort of round brush in a sense, it had big ball attached to it, a cast iron ball attached to it, on a big long rope, a chain or something like that. And that would be dropped down the chimney. He'd keep pumping it up and the weight would put it down. (James Baxter)

Lums (chimneys) set on fire on purpose or by accident sometimes brought the excitement of the Fire Brigade and a messy dousing:

And how you knew your chimney was needing swept, your fire used to smoke. You would get puffs of sooty smoke coming out. You could smell it. Our mother would say, 'Oh, I'll need to get the chimney swept, or the lum'll go on the fire.' Now there were some people who, either they couldn't afford to pay for the sweep or they didn't want to spend the money on the sweep, would set the lums on fire to clear them. And how they did that was they'd get a paper, a lighted paper, let it go up the chimney, and sure as fate you would hear the lum roaring, and then there would be sparks. The whole street would be blacked out with smoke, you know. And sometimes the fire raged quite awhile. And it could be a danger because these old houses, the wooden joists were always dried up, and it could have set them on fire.

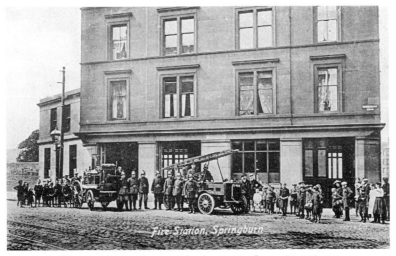

27. The Fire Brigade outside the Springburn Fire Station
c. 1910, with tenements above.

And sometimes somebody had to send for the Fire Brigade to come and put the hose down. When that happened, whoever's house got the hose down the chimney, the firemen didn't hesitate. They'd go up onto the roof and they'd just put the hose down the chimney and the person paid for their stupidity, you know [laugh]! Of course, they also got hell for bringing the Fire Brigade out, I don't know whether they were fined or not, or made to pay for it, I can't remember, but they might have because it was an unnecessary fire. (James Baxter)

7

Roon Oor Back

'When I went back years after to
see this back court I often wonder at the
things that took place in it.'

*The back court, or back, was a busy place. Some of the slightly better
tenements might have their own little grassy back green, but often
two closes, or three at a corner, would let into this communal area. It
widened the community of the close a little further, for all the back
windows looked over it and the neighbouring backs. This was an
essential 'service area', with its midden for rubbish, its shared wash-
house and place for drying clothes and beating carpets. Usually paved
over, it was a hard environment but a relatively safe place for close
children to play, and was always full of activity.*

THE WASH-HOUSE

'An' ye took yer bare feet and ye danced up and doon
on the blankets to take the dirt oot.'

*Doing the big weekly wash in the wash-house was one of the most
backbreaking of all the chores necessary to keep up a tenement
house. And again it involved a great deal of sharing and neighbourliness. Doing a wash today is quite a different matter.*

And, of course, washing wasn't done with a washing machine. You went down to the wash-house. Down at the back court.
Put on the boiler fire and all that sort of thing. You kind of forget
about these kind of things. I've done a washing this morning, for
example, but you wouldn't know a thing about it! (Margaret
Burnside)

Indeed for tenement mothers in those days it was usually a full day's work, starting with filling a huge copper boiler with a hose attached to a sink tap, and lighting the fire underneath several hours ahead of time to get the water eventually to the boil.

My mother, she was generally on a wash day up about half past five in the morning an' got the boiler started down in the back. The old wash-house. An' then came up and made the breakfast, and got us all tae school. And then went back down, finished her washin', then came up and did the rest of the cooking. (Sam Watt)

Annie Miller's family's turn came on a Friday, which was traditionally a heavy day for housework, as we've seen. Her mother often finished by candlelight – but that included putting the children through the wash too!

I can always seem to remember we had a Friday. And after my mother had done the washing it was usually eight, nine or ten o'clock at night, and there was no lights, of course. It was all candles. She had a couple of candles at each end of this big, oh, it was a massive place, and the washing was done. And then we all got turfed into this boiler. (Annie Miller)

Often a turn came less frequently than once a week, so neighbourly gestures were much appreciated.

Each had a wash-house, a great big wash-house. And you had the big boiler and big tubs. So clothes were maybe steeping the night before. You all took your turn you see. In fact, they gave you a card out and you knew your turn. It turned out once in every twelve days 'cause there were twelve neighbours in the stair. But sometimes a person wouldn't want to go in and you could get their turn.

What my mother did was, when the next person followed her, she would ask them did they want water left, and they would be only too glad. And they would go down and steep their clothes. Some maybe did them that night if they hadn't a lot, or wait till the next morning, you know. (Martha MacMillan)

This might be particularly welcome when there was a stream of baby's nappies to deal with, which otherwise had to be done in the house by hand.

Nappies were just washed every day. And she [mother] had a

28. The wash-house in the back court. The brick stacks
built onto the back of the tenements behind are the shared
toilets on the stair landings.

pail and it had a top, a lid on it that she put them into, with disinfectant or something, till she could battle the lot. For she had to wash them at the sink with a scrubbing board, and an Acme wringer that you turned the handle. And if she could get out, if it was dry, she'd put them out in the back court. For ye just had your day for the wash-house. You couldn't go every day. But a lot of the time, neighbours who would use the wash-house would come to my mother and offer her when they were done 'Would you like to use the water?' It was a good big boiler of soapy water left. And my mother would thankfully take the chance. It probably wasn't very hygienic. You'd think that might not be very hygienic, because others' washing had been washed in it. But my mother was delighted. She took every chance. (Marion Smith)

With pressure on the wash-house and the time it took to heat up the water some people would take their wash to the 'steamie', the public wash-house. But this wasn't exactly an easy way out, unless you lived close, though it was a sociable place to work. It was usually accomplished by piling the wash on top of an old pram.

She would walk away over a mile away with her big washin' like a tinker ... goin' down to that place where you washed them [the steamie]! Well it wasn't so bad goin' down. But walking back up 'cause they'd be wet they'd be heavy you know! (Malcolm Law)

Ye could go tae the wash-house in Kay Street, but it was just the same, hand washin'. I mean, no machinery then, it was all done with a washin' board. The only thing was when ye wrung your clothes out, ye put them on tae these, what they termed 'drying horses'. An' they were put in an' it half-dried your clothes. Ye were only allowed in so long. (Agnes Muirhead)

The wash-house contained large sinks and a wringer or mangle to squeeze the water out of the washing before it was hung up in the back court on ropes stretched across and attached to an iron hook, and forked up high off the ground with a long pole. These ropes could also hold carpets to be beaten. When clothes were taken inside, the ropes were taken down, wound round elbow and hand, and put away with the pegs for the next wash-day. Pegs incidentally were often beautifully made of polished wood. If it was raining, as it often did and does in Glasgow, the damp wash had to be 'humped' up the stair and hung on the pulley, the clothes horse, the mantelpiece, and sometimes over the back of chairs placed at the fire to let things dry.

Washing was not a solitary occupation however. Neighbours would stop in for a chat, and children ran back and forth, and were sometimes enlisted to help.

29. A boy outside a back-court midden c. 1910. Some children went barefoot from choice in the summer.

Aye well, when my mother was doing blankets she used to say, 'Charlie, John, c'm 'ere.' And ye went up on the tub. Not the tub they were boiling. The cool tub. An' ye took your bare feet and ye danced up and doon on the blankets to take the dirt oot. Aye, that's what they done. (Charles McCaig)

With children involved, there were the inevitable mishaps and dramas, as Sam Watt relates:

An' about six o'clock in the morning you had to get up and stoke the fire an' get a good heat so as the boiler would be warm enough. One time ma sister went down, stoked the fire, put a big fire on, and she came up. An' we were all sitting with oor breakfast. An' there were a big 'BOOM'! She never put water in the boiler! It blew up! Aye! We'd away to get a new boiler. It blew the boiler tae bits. It was a good job there was nobody in!

... You washed your clothes in the tubs. Then there was this big boiler. In fact, a story about that. I'm lucky I managed to be here. I was only maybe a lad aboot four year old or that. An' ma mother was doing the washing. An' I was running aboot the back. An' I went into the wash. There was a stool at the boiler for maybe a wee person tae stand up, so I climbed up on the stool and pulled myself up an' toppled in. I know my mother came in at that time. She saw ma ankles sticking oot, an' pulled me oot! She just got me in time, an' that was it! (Sam Watt)

BACK-COURT CONFLICTS

'I got the woman! I got her intae the back close and
I walloped her wi' the carpet beater! I did!'

Of course there were among the tenements unhappy families which bred insecure children and eventually difficult adults. Among the tolerant and friendly neighbours so warmly remembered there were some thorny ones. While stair neighbours normally stuck together, there could be feuds with those from adjacent closes and backs.

Agnes Muirhead says she had a difficult neighbour to deal with in the early 1930s, but had learned to stand her ground when she was young because, raised by her grandmother until returning to live with her parents, she was picked upon by playmates – so 'I'd always have to stand on my own two feet ... I had to defend myself!' When her mother had trouble with a neighbour causing smoke to blacken her clean wash, Agnes soon sorted her out:

This day, it must have been my half day off. And my mother had been washin' when I came in. I said, 'What's the matter?' I'm after puttin' out a washin'. Would ye have a look at that?' I said, 'What is it?' She said, 'That's them settin' the papers up the chimneys.' I said, 'What dae ye mean, settin' the papers up the chimneys?' She says, 'That's every time ye put a washin' out here!' I said, 'Oh, is it?' So I cut through tae the wash-house, and I cops this woman at the wash-house door. I said, 'Excuse me, who set the wash-house on fire?' 'Who wants tae know?' I said, 'I do'. 'It's oor wash-house, and if we want tae set it on fire, we'll set it on fire.' I says, 'Just do that. But the next time you put out a washin' ye'll have tae take it in.' 'Why?' she says. I says, 'Tae re-wash it.'

So I went tae the neighbour up the stair and I says tae her, 'Do you get you washin' dirty?' She says, 'Agnes, it's terrible here, you've no idea what we're made tae put up with.' I said, 'Is that a fact?' She says, 'That's right.' I says, 'Right, what day do they do their washin'?' 'A Monday.' I says, 'Right, I'll have a Monday off.' I *did* take a Monday off my work. The washin' went out. It was coal fires at the time. I says tae Katie Tinley, 'You have a bucket o' ashes ready.' She says, 'Right.'

Well, where oor ash pits was, their back was open. So I went out with the ash bins. [Smack!] Right intae the back-green ash bins. But the dust went right intae their clothes. They came out! I says, 'Told ye ye would need tae take your washin' in, didn't I? And every time my mother's tae do a double washin' you'll dae one along wi' her!' So that stopped that. We put an end tae that.

Agnes Muirhead also had trouble over carpet-beating: this account gives an interesting glimpse of the policing of the back courts.

Well, one time there was a back, a wall, between the buildings. Now, at that time it wasn't fitted carpets: ye'd a fire-side carpet and ye had a carpet over at your sideboard and ye had a carpet up the centre o' your hall. Now, ye took these carpets out maybe twice a week an' beat them an' brushed them. So we used the wall for throwin' the carpets over. So I was out this night and I was beatin' away at the carpets here and the carpet kept comin' back over on me! I thought it was a kid that was at the other side o' the wall. I said, 'Look, throw that carpet over again I'll jump this wall!' And the carpet came over an' I jumped the wall. I got the woman! I got her intae the back close and I walloped her wi' the carpet beater! I did! Och, I didnae wallop her sore. I let her know, that she wouldnae push us. So I comes back up.

The next thing the door goes. A tenant. 'Agnes, Agnes!' I says, 'What?' She says, 'Noo, remember,' she says, 'Ye weren't out doin' carpets.' I says, 'How, what's the matter?' She says, 'That's the police away up that stair. That woman sent for the police.' Police never came near that door. I don't know how many doors they went tae, but they never come tae mine, because the woman didnae know who I was. I don't think she'd ever seen me before.

But any road, the same tenant and I were out in the back, I'll no' mention any names, and we're on the railin's at the top, we weren't near the dyke, and we were beatin' carpets. And I seen the flashlight coming through the close. I said, 'Here's somebody with a flashlight.' And I looked up. Two policemen! They came right up, 'What dae ye think your doing'?' I said, 'Ye see what we're doing, beating carpets.' 'Are you aware you're over your time?' I said. 'What, at seven o'clock at night?' He says, 'Yes.' I said, 'I never knew there was a limited time tae beat carpets.' So he just looked at me. He said, 'I don't want any cheek offa you.' I said, *'Look! I didn't know there was a limited time fur beatin' carpets!'* 'Well,' he says, 'We've had a report about you out beatin' carpets, all 'oors at night.' I said, 'No, no, we come oot Tuesday an' Friday. Twice a week we come oot at the same time an' beat the carpets.' 'Well', he says, 'You won't beat carpets after six o'clock.' I said, 'Who'll no?' he said, 'You.' I said, 'Oh yes I will,' I says, 'I don't stop my work till six o'clock.' I said, 'By the time I come home here, it's half past six, by the time I get a cuppa tea it's seven o'clock, an' that's the only time I have for beatin' carpets, try an' stop me, try an' stop me!' I said, 'An' I'll beat ma carpets at seven o'clock, Tuesday an' Friday or Wednesday an' Friday an' you'll no stop me.' He said, 'I've a good mind tae take you inside.' I says, 'Jist you do that.' Never said another word, he jist moved away, because I knew I was in the right. I'll tell ye why I knew!

My father was a miner, an' he came in one night, he told us this himself. He came in one night, he was in the back shift, two tae ten. An' he came in, an' he'd the window open and he was lyin' over the window, ye know; it was in the summertime. Policeman came along, 'Do you mind getting in out the window?' 'It's my own house I'm in.' 'I don't care whose house, ye've no right lyin' oot yir windy at this time o' the night.' I mean there was restrictions then that are no out now. He says, 'I'm just in from my work.' 'I don't care whether ye are or no.'

So when he went in the next day, he spoke tae the foreman in the mines before he had lifted his lamp. He said, 'Listen, when you leave here at ten o'clock, you have up tae two o'clock in the mornin' tae lie out your window for fresh air.' Father says, 'Right.' So they came back down ... So they were gonnae charge him. He says, 'Just make a charge.' See the minute they heard he wis a miner, that wis the charge dropped. So I knew I wis within my rights on the back court. (Agnes Muirhead)

WINDOWS

'That's the half-past eight singers. You'd better get
away and get on the tram.'

Windows looking over the back court and the street gave easy and informal contact with family, neighbours and the wider community. The back windows were being constantly opened: to shout down to children in the back court to come up for their tea, for instance. Or to respond to 'Mammy, throw us doon a piece an' jam!', with a slice of bread spread with a little margarine and strawberry jam, put in a poke (a brown paper bag), and 'chucked oot the windy'. Money wrapped in a piece of paper could descend the same way with shouted instructions to a child to run for a loaf of bread or a newspaper. Anyone up to mischief could be reprimanded from above: 'If you don't stop chalking on that wall I'm gonnae tell your Mammy on you' – and in those days, the child would usually stop!

'Hingin' oot the windy' was a favourite posture for general relaxing observation of the outside world – though disapproved of among the most respectable. And back-court windows flung up and slammed down were also useful for the occasional argument, where insults could be shouted back and forth in complete safety.

The back court was often a place of entertainment, used for staging back-court concerts by children, or for more informal gatherings.

Och ye could nearly all sing you know ... It was part of their life, singing. Even the men, the older blokes, they must have been twenty up to thirty: I can remember in the summer nights they used to sit round the back. It was a grass back. It was quite, it appeared to be quite big, but again as I say, when I went back years after to see this back court I often wonder at the things that took place in it. But they used to sit around the back harmonisin' and that. Great singing, so it was, and this seemed to be something we all inherited – no' necessary doin' solos, but community type singin', like part of your life. (John Wotherspoon)

The window to the back court also allowed entertainers to serenade the houses for a few coppers tossed down in charity. Some came regularly as clockwork. Marion Smith's mother used to mark the time by the back-court singers:

There was a huge sort of 'character', I think that is the best word to describe him. He came round and sang regularly in the back courts. Monday morning she'd say, 'That's the half-past-eight singers. You'd better get away and get on the tram.'

And there was a man and his wife. He had lost his sight, and he sang beautifully, and then he finished up with a little speech, saying, 'The loss of the eyesight's a terrible loss. It's only those that are affected that really know the void.' My mother would get two coppers, two pennies, and roll them in a piece of newspaper and throw them out. Everyone seemed to do that, no matter how little they had, they could always spare a copper for the blind man. (Marion Smith)

People were willing to be entertained by watching other people, and their windows mitigated against loneliness. Many had interesting outlooks. Margaret Burnside remembers the panoramic view from her upper-storey tenement windows in the 1920s.

Oh, we had a great outlook! On Saturdays my father was always working and one of the things that mother liked to do was sit at the room window and do her knitting. And she was very good at knitting or reading. She'd look up and watch all the folk going up to the park because there was a trail of folk always on a Saturday, winter or summer and Sundays too. And, of course, my father worked every second Sunday. My mother used to watch the folk. In the summertime it was great. Our back window was super because it looked right across to the west. On a clear day you could actually see the island of Arran.

It used to be said that a drunk man got into a tramcar one day and asked for a ticket to heaven. And the conductor says, 'Och, aye! We'll take you to Springburn, it's the nearest place you'll get.' The outlook was terrific. It was great. (Margaret Burnside)

Small boys interested in trains, trams, and machinery often had fascinating views from their windows:

We lived across from what used to be Cowlairs works in Gourlay Street, two or three closes away before you came to the railway bridge. You'd sit at the windy and watch the trains go up and doon. And we knew the times and places of every train [that] went out round about that way. Sat and watched the trains go up, it was a fascinating wonder ... Aye, it was a great place to live! (James Vaughan)

30. Springburn was built around trains. This is the Cowlairs Incline overlooked by the tenements of Keppochhill Road.

You could see everything that was passing down the main road, so it was good that way. Because I was fond of tramcars and things like that. On a wet day you could look out a window and see them. (Douglas McMillan)

I always minded, ma windows looked intae, I think it was the engine shop. It had big, big windows, big oval windows running along, an' it was a' belt driven. At night, the dark nights, it was lit up and you saw all these belts a' going round about. It was really interesting to look at it. (Sam Watt)

A window fronting on a street gave interaction with the wider community. In the 1930s Mr Dewar's grandmother gauged the passing of the seasons by the visibility of men going home.

And where we lived was between Springburn Road and
Keppochill road. And the Caley men used to cross to their homes
in crowds. And the Cowlairs men crossed our road to the other
side. So my grandmother used to go by the time when in Feb-
ruary she'd say 'That's the winter gettin' past. We can see the
Caley men now.' Because it was dark, there was no lights there.
(William Dewar)

31. The Orange Walk along Springburn Road, viewed
from a tenement window.

*Or there might be a view of processions in the main streets – pipe
bands or the Orange Walk remembered here in the 1930s.*

There was the Orange walk. They used to come up, and I
remember my sister, she was a tomboy. She hauled me down to
Springburn Road to see the fights! I was scared, she wasn't.
There was plenty of fights in Springburn Road at the Orange
Walk. Later on, all the Orange Men came to Springburn Park
and it really was a sight to see them all marching up Broomfield
Road. It took hours for them to pass it really did. Of course we
could see them from the living room window. (Sam Watt)

8

Doing the Shopping

'When we came up to Springburn in 1932, oh,
I thought I was in heaven, 'cause it was actually
wonderful. It had a shopping centre.'

*As Mary Williamson remembers, shopping in Springburn before the
war was easy. Many people look back with nostalgia to this aspect of
life, for shopping was an important social activity, taking people
beyond the world of close and back. One of the things most lamented
today is the clearing away of all the shops and the busy street life
that went with them. Shops stayed open long hours, and along with
the cinemas and dance-halls, made the community self-sufficient.
The tenements of the main streets incorporated shops large and
small on their ground floors, lining the streets with variety.*

THE SHOPS ON THE STREET

'Stevenson the grocer ... allowed customers
weekly credit and gave you a poke of sweets when
you settled your account.'

*Many things could be bought in the close from the numerous
hawkers who came round the streets, like the tripe man with his
horse-drawn cart (who came round on Sundays with buttermilk);
or the hand-pushed barrel delivering milk before the days of bottles.*

And your milk was delivered by this bloke wi' the cart ... And
it used to be just like the big milk can. And you opened the tap
and held your jug under it and filled it. (John Wotherspoon)

*Shopping was a daily activity to buy fresh food and replace stores
as they were needed – for there was no weekly supermarket shop, no*

117

stacking of freezers with convenience foods. Children were often sent out to do the 'messages': they could safely ask someone to take them across the road, and they would be known at the shop.

We would very often go to the well-known grocer, Gavin McMillan. We would go for our messages and ended up going out with a wee chocolate wafer biscuit. Now in those days, the biscuit's price was actually a farthing, so it was quite something to go out for your messages and come out with a chocolate wafer biscuit in your hand. (James Vaughan)

But serious shopping was almost exclusively a women's activity. Shopkeepers would know their customers by name, and they in turn would be loyal to 'their' butcher, grocer and so on. Window-shopping was a pleasurable Saturday pastime too.

I mean you could go out, it was a regular thing to go out on a Saturday afternoon. The men were at football matches of course, and you would walk up Springburn Road on one side window-shopping or shopping, and cross over at the terminus and walk down the other side. You could put in your whole Saturday afternoon doing that. What could you do now? Everything is absolutely gone. That's dreadful. I mean you could walk

32. Fine window display at Cochrane's grocers,
547 Springburn Road, in 1934.

through Hoey's at the corner of Gourlay Street, you could walk through the Co-operative from top to bottom. (Agnes McDonald)

Marion Smith's astonishing powers of recall come to the fore again as she remembers all the shops on her street around the time of the First World War. Her account shows clearly how the shops contributed to a strong sense of community.

These are the shops etcetera as I remember them, starting from our corner of Gourlay Street and Miss Gibson's shop. She was a kindly, if rather severe, maiden lady. She sold sweets and jotters and slate pencils and thimbles for the sewing classes and cotton sacks and things.

Then there was our close and the next one, and next came the magnificent Princes Cinema, complete with commissionaire in uniform. My mother and father had a weekly date there. In these days there was, in addition to the Pathe News Gazette, an on-going serial, each episode ending in a 'cliff hanger' to lure you back next week, a drama of some sort, and a comedy.

Next to the Princes Cinema was the butcher's shop run by big Davie Newton. Here we stood for hours for some meat. These queues became quite social occasions, much gossip being dispensed (not the malicious kind) to lighten the weary wait. Then there was Sancroft's newsagents, an ice cream shop, Young's Dairy, which had the best scones and the most delicious potted meat I've ever tasted. There was a large double windowed grocer's next, but we didn't really patronize them. It was run by two brothers of a sort of melancholy cast of feature, a bit off putting. They did have beautiful large canisters in their shop, sort of black lacquer with gold and red trim, but it was not a shop we frequented.

Then the 'Eureka Vaults', a public house, outside of which the Salvation Army played on a Saturday night their lovely rousing music. We all stood on the fringes and out came the men from the pub, to be cajoled into tossing any loose change onto the big drum. 'Another penny to make the shilling', coaxed the Army captain, and when it went over the shilling, of course it started all over again.

There was Parkin's fruit barrow at Palermo Street and on Saturday late canny shoppers like my mother could get great

33. Alexander Whitecross, a family butcher's shop on
Gourlay Street, in the 1930s.

bargains as they couldn't keep the fruit and veg over the weekend in those days.

Turning the corner at the Eureka Vaults into Springburn
Road you had Stevenson the grocer, who allowed customers
weekly credit and gave you a poke of sweets when you settled
your account.

There was a Waddell's shop that sold cooked meats and had a
large ashet of salmon paste in the window. This paste was a
violent pink in colour and I now shudder to think what was in it,
but it was a passion of mine – I loved the taste.

Oliver Early the Jewellers came next, then the bank, and now
we were at Cowlairs Road. From then on the Co-op dominated
the rest of Springburn Road up to Angus Street, Angus Street,
where we stood again in queue when the Co-op dividend was
paid out. We were sure to get a penny from mum that day . . .

One other remarkable shop was at the end of our street,
opposite corner to the Eureka Vaults. An emporium, no less, run
by Sam Hoey, consisting of many departments. Lots of Springburn girls left school and went into Hoey's. They had a cash

34. Mrs Sancroft, proprietor of Sancroft's newsagent's, 12
Gourlay Street, with her sons, in 1923.

system. A rail ran from the counter to a cashier in a glass edifice
above. A series of wooden balls were unscrewed and your cash
and your bill put inside, then the other half screwed back on, and
a jerk on a cord by the girl sent the wooden ball spinning away to
the cashier up above. She put your change back in the ball and
screwed it together and sent it spinning back to the counter. I
could have watched this for hours. When I was applying for a
chance to sit the examination for a job in the City Chambers I
filled in the form and then saw it had to be signed by a J.P.
[Justice of the Peace]. No trouble, my dad said, 'Sam Hoey will
sign it', and he did, but I was quaking at having to approach this
illustrious being. (Marion Smith)

*The illustrious being's son recalls more matter-of-factly a system
which fascinated young and old alike:*

We had a central cash point with a pneumatic, a 'Lamson'
pneumatic tube system and the brass canisters that went in and
we had usually three or four girls in that, in the cash desk, who
handled the cash, basically and handled cheques. It was a highly
efficient system in its own way too. (S. Graham Hoey)

THE CO-OPERATIVE AND HOEY'S

'I don't think half the people would
have survived without the Co-operative ... The
Co-operative was a constant lifeline.'

The big shops, Hoey's (founded in 1886), and especially the Co-operative (opened in 1831), dominate memories of shopping in Springburn throughout this period.

Springburn was a good shopping centre. You could get everything there from the Co-operative, especially your bed linen, men's underwear, and good shoes. Carpeting – in those days, you know, you bought a fireside rug or a big carpet. It sold furniture. You could almost get anything. Then Hoey's was a nice furniture [shop] – well not so much furniture then as what they did eventually, but menswear and ladies' wear and bed linen, you know. Good shops then in Springburn. (Margaret Patrick)

The Co-operative movement had an enormous influence on ordinary people's lives at this period. Its great benefit was paying dividends on purchases, which were often used as savings; and allowing credit which could be essential to family economy.

The Co-operative book played a big part. I don't think half the people would have survived without the Co-operative, you know. I think eventually the people must have cleared their debt as the family grew up ... but the Co-operative was a constant lifeline. (Ina Wotherspoon)

Oh yes, that was where you shopped. I mean everybody – well, when we were young – [shopped in] the Co- operative, and then when I was married, I was always in there. That's where you got all your stuff, you know, the Co-operative. You got a club card out, you know? You paid so much: if it was a twenty pound club you paid, oh it was twenty shillings, it'd be a pound a week for twenty weeks. Oh yes, it was a lovely shop. (Mary Urquhart)

Clothes were always a bit of a problem though my mother was very good at making things. But for anything practical it was the Co-op Club, paying a shilling in the pound, and the numbers being drawn weekly so you could perhaps get your club line early and then a visit to the drapery or the shoe department. The Co-op was a godsend. (Marion Smith)

This system, called a 'menage', for speeding the acquisition of major purchases was sometimes run privately by a neighbour, either for a small commission paid by the women in the group, or for a reward from Hoey's or the Co-operative.

She would get twenty women interested, they would pay her two shillings a week. She would put cards marked 1 to 20 in a hat and women who were in the menage would each pick a number out of the hat and that was the number of the week she would get her two pounds. The lady who run the menage would get a pair of towels or something for her efforts from the store. (Sam Watt)

William McGinlay who started work in the Cowlairs Co-operative as a message boy in 1926 at the age of twelve and worked there for many years explains the dividend and share system.

Your dividend was declared at the end of the three months and if it was 2/3d to the pound which most of the time it was, then you'd get your two-and-threes declared according to the purchases – if you'd thirty [pounds' worth] then it was thirty times 2/3d you got, and if you felt as if you could leave it lying, then you put it into your shares. (William McGinlay)

As Agnes McDonald recalls, the Co-op's empire spread throughout Springburn, as it did through other towns; and she was one who put her dividend to good use.

The Co-operative had their own butcher's shop, their own fish shop, their own baker's shop, their own chemist's, their own furniture store, their own draper's store, their own optician's, and every wee part of Springburn there would be another grocer's, another dairy belonging to the Co-op. On Petershill Road there was a Co-operative fish shop and a clothes shop. There is not a single Co-operative shop of any kind now in Springburn, not one.

Some people would lift their dividends in order to pay rent, and I mean the dividends from the Co-operative were back-up. I mean we were a monthly rent so it didn't affect me in this way, but there was people around the corner from me were quarterly rents and any of them that I was friendly with they would lift their Co-operative dividend and go and pay their rent to the factor. I never. It was an awful struggle to do it, mind you, but I never lifted my dividend.

And the dividend when I was there, was 2/10d to the pound. You used to save that up, oh yes, I saved that up for two or three quarters an' I got quite a few pounds . . . I bought various things, one day I bought a, an' I have still got it, a nice sideboard. I got it in the Co, the big Co, over at, near Paisley Road Toll, that lovely big Co where all the furniture is. The Co's furniture was always very good, so I bought that, I bought that sideboard an' a beautiful – I've still got it – a lovely china cabinet; an' I bought that in the Co too, with my dividend money, dear, but I saved it up all through the years you see . . . the dividends were colossal! (Agnes McDonald)

Another great advantage apart from credit was that a woman could take things on approval, so that men who wouldn't go shopping could try clothes on at home.

With the store book you got things on credit: you got your food on credit an' you got goods on credit throughout the weeks and paid it either at the end of the week or the end of the month or whatever. They had a great thing that you could get things out on approval, so you could go and get boots and shoes or a pair of trousers or whatever and you could bring them back to the house and either the man of the house or whatever could try them on, see whether they fitted them, and if you were satisfied with them then you would go and say, 'Right, I want to purchase them'.

It was commonly believed that the Co-op helped control the price of food in the community. It also ran various welfare schemes for those on very low incomes, including convalescent homes.

Yes and I'd say this, with the Co-op, I think they helped to control the prices of food because the private trade waited till the Co-op made their figure before they put out theirs, you see, and if the Co-op put out an article at, say, 10d, they would cut it maybe to 9½d, you see. If the Co-op hadn't been there to do that, they'd – well I think it shows up now, the way the prices are going up – they've not got some big opposition that's keeping them. Well, that's my attitude and I think it's a point that's worth mentioning, you know.

Well, for anybody that was in dire circumstances, well they could write in to Cowlairs Co and they would get a benefit. It would maybe be in the form of a voucher to purchase grocery goods, maybe up to five pounds, you see. I think this originated during the General Strike, away back years ago when people were so hard up: the Cowlairs Co gave out vouchers in those days for food.

Well, even when I was working, I got them in and I was an apprentice – no, I was a grocer, a full-time grocer – £3 2s 6d I was getting and these people were getting a voucher for Cowlairs for a fiver: now that was like two weeks' wages, you know.

They had their homes for the customers. If you'd been ill and produced your doctor's line that you'd been ill, really ill, you could have a week or a fortnight at, maybe at Largs or Galashiels, and they'd another one, I think, at Dunoon. There were three or four homes. But they got that and all they did was pay their own fare. It was a beautiful hotel that one at Largs, oh yes. I was down visiting it one day and it was beautiful – oh it was like a first-class hotel! Oh, they got their meals and the people said that the meals were marvellous; oh yes, it was very good. (William McGinlay)

However not everyone could afford to be a member of the Co-op:

Mother couldn't afford to be you see. Although we'd a big family well Mother was a good cook, she could make the likes of pancakes, things like that – there were lots of things she just couldn't afford. You had to have money to really be able to shop in the Co-operative. (Martha MacMillan)

There was a political and a social angle too: Mary Tourish and her mother were members of the Co-operative Guild. To be a member, you were supposed to accept the tenets of the Labour Party, but there were plenty of Tories in it for the social life it offered.

Well, my mother was in the Co-operative Guild for years and then I became involved, and I was only six months in it when I was asked to be the secretary, but it was a case of nobody would take the job so I took it. And then I was President for four years, I was President [of] Petershill Co-operative Guild, then we amal-

gamated with Central Guild. Petershill was a great Guild, smashing. Then I was only an ordinary member and then I gradually
got put onto committees and then ended up as President again.

Well it was just speakers on different functions of the Co-
operative that used to come, the likes of the bakers, and soft
drinks, and we had political speakers as well . . . Before you could
get into committees you had to have a certain purchasing power
. . . you also had to accept the rules of the Labour Party in the
Co-operative. A friend of mine . . . wouldn't accept it, and she
was a very proficient speaker and very clever and she was barred
from the committee because she wouldn't take the oath, as it
were. And what used to rile me was the fact that I knew there
were Tories sittin' beside me who accepted the oath but they'd
no intentions of carryin' it out, you know, but as long as they
had the purchasin' power, so much per quarter buying power,
then they were allowed into the committee.

It was a social life for them and somewhere for them to go and
they were interested in the Guild as a social life cause in these
days they didn't have the Bingo, and they loved the Guild. Once
a month we had a dance and we had hot pie and peas and a wee
dance. And we had speakers or somebody comin' demonstrating
to us. In fact a lot of the women who went to the Guild, that was
when they first learned politics, was at the Co-operative Guild.
(Mary Tourish)

*William McGinlay gives a fascinating account of the grocery
department of the Cowlairs Co-op between the wars, underlining the
enormous difference in the selling of provisions in days when most
came into the shops in bulk and had to be weighed and packaged,
'made up', on the premises. Display skills were very important. And
of course, there was no refrigeration.*

Well, you would stock shelves and, you know, make up stock.
You were always making up stock in the grocers' shops. Made
up your barley, peas, lentils and all rice type of thing – all came
in loose and you would help one of the grocers. You would fill up
the bags and he would weigh them and another one would fold
them off . . . You never had pre-packed sugar in the shops . . . Of
course you never displayed sugar because it was just brown
paper bags: there was no brand names then, and the same with

all your cereals, you know, they were all brown paper bags.

Hundredweight bags for cereals, then two-hundredweight bags for sugar, and they were heavy for us to move around, you know! You made up your cheese, you made up everything, you know, butter – marg came in made up, but butter came in in bulk, you know. You made up your hundredweight cask of butter and you cut it with a wire and all that, made it up, packed it on the marble slabs. You made the cheese up in half-pounds, quarters and pounds on the Thursday and that would do you until Saturday. Cheeses, aye, you used to display them. Sometimes you would cut them in two, you know, a cheese in two and show it in the window but you had to take it out at night so's it wouldn't dry up, you see. The butter in the summer, you just couldn't make up too much each night. In the morning you'd make up as much as would do that day and that's all. It was as cool a place as you could get in the shop you kept your butter, you know.

35. Mary Maclean serving in the Cowlairs Co-operative, 1932.

Hams, all your hams you'd to bone and skin those, roll your hams ... And you'd have about twenty bacons or hams up there, all faced up lovely, what you called faced up. And there'd be two on each board and there were skewers through them and then a customer would go out to the window and say, 'I'll have that one' or 'A half pound of that'. And you'd take it down from the window and cut for them, you know, and you also had some made up, ready cut, so that if they weren't fussy, they just took what we [had pre-cut], if it was nicely placed, or you displayed it. You could display a ham that looked lovely, you know, even although maybe a bit of fat on it, you could have it looking beautiful, you see. Especially bacon ... if it was displayed, it made a far better [impression], you sold far more.

You could get barley, peas, rice, split peas, lentils – they knew they could get that, you always could get that in a grocer's shop. They were always kept in drawers, you know, you pulled the drawer out for a one pound, a half pound, whatever they wished.

We had coffee, we had cloves, we had cayenne pepper, we had different types of pepper, we had ... crystallized fruit and things like that, you know. We didn't grind coffee in our shop. It came in ground in bags and we sold it loose, the same as pepper. It was sold loose in those days, too, pepper – they were all sold loose. Tobacco was rolled up, made up in the shop. We used to get big rolls of it – thick black tobacco and you'd make it up and weigh it out and you'd special scales for them because it was such small amounts. Oh, they were all brass scales. For the sugar they would weight up to fourteen pounds, ye see – well they turned slower than your scales for your tobacco which were very, very accurate.

There were very few people used ground coffee in those days. As a matter of fact, in those days, it was mostly all Camp coffee, you know, the liquid coffee and chicory. There wasn't – well, coffee was coming in before the war, right enough, you know, ground coffee and Nescafé was there, but it was never as popular, you know. It wasn't till the war and after the war that ground coffee and the jars came in as much. (William McGinlay)

Hoey's shared with the Co-operative the trade in supplying overalls, boots and 'bunnets' (caps) for the working man. Here is another mention of a 'menage':

The Co-operative and Hoey's had departments for works, they stocked everything. Boots, tackety boots, overalls, all the different overalls, and tools.

When I was an apprentice they used to do, the Shop Committee would run, what they called a menage. It was a shilling a week, understand, a shilling a week, and your turn came up, you got a pound, and you took the pound to the Co-operative, and ... that's how you built your tool kit up. Co-operative and Hoey's. Hoey's didn't supply tools, Co-operative supplied tools, they had a big Ironmongery. The shops catered for the works, because that was where they were getting their money from.

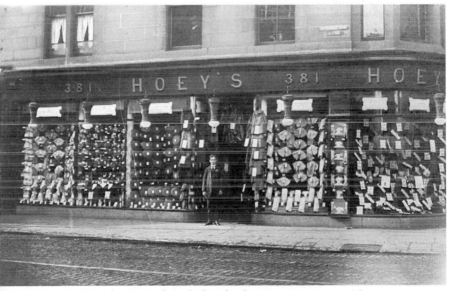

36. Hoey's, Springburn's family department store, with its men's caps conveniently next to the door, in the 1920s.

Graham Hoey's amusing account of the embarrassment that some men experienced in being inside his family store emphasises how strongly shopping was felt to be a woman's task:

We had men's caps, for example. We'd an enormous trade in men's caps. The back door in Gourlay Street was a fascinating place to be because it entered straight into the men's department and the technique, if you were a man working in Springburn and wanted a new cap, was you came and opened the door and still keeping your hand on the handle of the door, you said, 'A bunnet', and somebody gave you one and you put it on your head and said, 'Aye, that's fine' and gave your 1/11d or whatever it was and got out the door as quickly as possible! They were terrified.

It was totally embarrassing, totally embarrassing. Nothing else was bought by a workman except that. The wife bought a semmit and drawers, wife bought socks for him, wife bought everything for him. He didn't like to be seen, so it was in the door, as I say, and we couldn't have the caps at the far end of the department, they had to be up at the door, so that they could just grab them, put them on their head and out again. It was quite an extraordinary state of affairs, when you think about it now! (S. Graham Hoey)

9

Weddings and Funerals

'Och, the only time you put on your old serge
suit was to go to a wedding or a funeral!'

*Weddings and more especially funerals were markers of the family's
place in a wider community. Funerals were the more important, and
it was commonly the whole neighbourhood that mourned. Weddings were generally modest events, though the practice of the
'scramble' for small coins tossed down by the best man outside the
church – when it could be afforded – made them popular with
children. Both occasions involved entertaining, normally in the
house, the relatives and friends of the individuals at the centre of the
events, and contributions from neighbours were again often relied
upon to ease the burden of the expense.*

WEDDINGS

'You got married ... And then you came back and your
mother gave you an old steak pie in the kitchen.'

*Marriages were simple affairs among most tenement families during
these years. Neighbours might donate a few extra eggs or a plate of
scones for a wedding breakfast, and a meal for the immediate family
and friends might be laid on by the parents of the bride. While in
higher social classes weddings could entail the furnishing of whole
houses at this period, most tenement newly-weds did not expect
much, as this matter-of-fact description from the 1930s makes
clear:*

You got married. You went to the vestry and the minister
married you, or if you were Catholic you went and the priest

married you. And then you came back and your mother gave you an old steak pie in the kitchen in our own house. Just the family. Maybe a few friends that gave you a cream and sugar or a pair of dishtowels. You were lucky if you got a pair of towels! Oh ye didnae get fridges then, you were lucky if ye had a house! (Mary Preece)

Families that were better off would make more of a splash, perhaps hiring a local hall and outside caterers, and arranging a small dance, as in the wedding of 1935 described below. Weddings during this period were often 'dry': the Temperance movement had a strong hold, especially on the parents' generation, which was not generally relaxed until after the social upheaval of the Second World War. Women of the respectable working class did not habitually drink or smoke at social occasions anyway.

Well weddings, they were just the usual ... my big brother was married in the Masonic and the Co-operative done the party. Steak pie and tatties, and all that sort of stuff. The wee square Albert cake with ice on it, fruit cake. Then the wee dance after that. There was no drinking at oor wedding! (John McKee)

During the times of high unemployment in the 1930s all the traditions had to be skimped, with some unfortunate consequences:

Och, they wir getting married on the dole! One woman got a ring an' she was showing it around. A beautiful gold ring! An' she was married. 'Oh what a beautiful gold ring!' A week later she couldnae get it off her finger. Her finger was jet black. He had bought it oot o' Woolworths. 'Cause they wir all poor, they couldnae buy things.

Another wedding, there was quite a few guests. There was tumblers, wee totie tumblers. There was wee tumblers an' big tumblers. This was at the reception ... So naturally all the men grabbed all the big tumblers [filled with ginger]. Cheers! But what they didnae know, the man was poor. He only had whisky in the wee tumblers. And we were all grabbing the biggest. Cheers! An' a' the women wir gettin' whisky, ye know! (Charles McCaig)

Weddings during the Second World War, as during the First, were often rushed affairs.

He done his time in the navy. He came home one Saturday.

37. Wedding portrait of Georgina and William Kemlo, 1920.
Best clothes were more usual wear than special white dresses.

'Are you going to be ma best man?' I says, 'You've gave me a rare bit of time.' He says, 'Quick I've got the minister. We're up in the church at the top Springburn Road.' And the guy came out, and these days, and they called your bans out in the street, ye know. The minister came out and you stood at his side and he shouted out 'David Carnegie's getting married to so and so.' This was it. 'Any objection?' And he called them out to people passing by. And that was your bans called. And he got married in the afternoon. And went in tae town at night. You got a few drinks and something to eat, and that was it! He was away in the Monday back! (Sam Watt)

It was a frantic time you see, you just grabbed your chances when you could. You couldn't plan ahead . . . my wife was under twenty-one, I was just twenty-one. Her parents were dead, and she had no proof, she didn't have their death certificates because it was a big sort of mixed family. Because she was under twenty-one she had to have parental consent. I went to the register office in Manchester trying to find out where these people were buried. We eventually got proof that way, and special licence. Bang! Then I got a train . . . and I got married, and I spent my honeymoon sitting in Leeds Station with my wife . . . and the next thing I knew we were in Blackpool with a draft, waiting for a boat. (Robert Lister)

Parents had generally more say about marriages during this period, when it was still expected that a young man at least inform the girl's parents of his intentions. In some families marriage would have been inconceivable without parental approval.

So my mother was with us actually when we went to pick the engagement ring. As long as my father was for it. If my father hadn't been for it, I wouldn't, no matter how much I loved that man. I wouldn't have got married without my father's say. But he did. So we had quite a nice wedding! (Amelia Newton)

While mother might be expected to be more intimate with a daughter, it seems that it commonly fell to the father to explain the facts of life – at the eleventh hour in the case of this eighteen-year-old married during the Second World War:

When I got married, it's a thing I don't tell many people, but on my wedding night, we went to the Empire Theatre actually, and we came back home. The room was given to us, which meant that my sister was married by that time. And there was *no way* I was going to sleep with that man that I had just married! *No way* was I going to sleep with a man [laugh]! So it finished up that night that I learned the facts of life! For my father had to take me in to that room and sit and talk. I mean, I was eighteen years of age. So that's when I learned.

Peggy Taylor, married at twenty-four in 1928, was better prepared for married life. But again it fell to her father to explain:

[Laugh] My father did, not my mother! Everyone thinks it's a scream, my father telling me the facts of life. I was brought up more like a tomboy than anything else. He could talk to me and he went and got all the books and told me to read them and then he explained it all to me. My mother was a very shy woman, you see. There's nobody shy nowadays, they get it at school now. (Peggy Taylor)

As we have seen, for many couples a celebratory night out stood in for a honeymoon. Houses were hard to find, and while some were fortunate enough to move into their own place, usually a single-end, many came home as man and wife to live, even if only temporarily, with relatives, or sometimes a neighbour who had space for lodgers: if there was no woman to keep house this could be a mutual advantage.

I remember coming back from ma honeymoon ... from Aberdeen. We had no house. We couldn't get a house. We stayed with an old fella. He was a widower. He had been a friend of us for years. And he gave us a room – he had a room and kitchen in the Blocks. And we stayed with him for about a year. And then we got a house from the fire brigade.

Furnishing a home was a slow business unless there was a wind-fall from a relative emigrating, or other help from the family.

We had a room and kitchen ... Don't laugh when I tell ye. We just shut the room door 'cause we didnae have it furnished. And if we had anybody comin' we carted our chairs from the kitchen into the room [laugh]. (John Dowie)

Employers were an important source of wedding presents, as in this account of the late thirties.

Ma husband worked in the bookies, and it was Tuck's the

bookie. And when we got married, as a wedding present he covered our floors with linoleum and, oh, a fireside rug he gave us. He also gave ma husband money for our wedding present, for our ring. Ma husband wasn't working at the time, to let you know. He was friendly with a lady that lived up the next close that got us the house. And she gave us a table and four chairs. And we got quite a number of wedding presents: pots and kettles and useful things. And, oh, I went up to the fruit shop and got two apple boxes ... we used to keep our shoes in them. And I made a curtain that went round them and a wee frill on the top. (Isabel Miller)

FUNERALS

'If it was so-and-so's death, it was everybody's death. Everybody mourned. You'd never see a curtain open or a window up. And there was a great sense of community.'

Funerals were observed with solemnity, and were often a moving expression of community feeling. Most families lost menfolk during the First World War. While the death of grandparents and parents was a natural enough loss to face, many interviewees recalled with intense feeling the loss in childhood of brothers or sisters, or even worse, perhaps, of their own child. When causes were given, they were usually such things as meningitis, influenza or one of the other infectious diseases which are discussed in the last chapter.

Most people died in their homes, and the body was kept in the house until the funeral. Sleeping in the same room as the coffin might sound gruesome today, but as this tender account shows it could ease the pain of parting with a loved one.

When my father died, he was in the room there, the coffin was in there. It didn't bother ye. Ye slept in there. And every so often, people would come up. And ye'd go in and see him. And ye'd be in the kitchen, and every so often you'd go in and have a wee look at him. In fact it was very touching to do it like that. Because it was just like he was lying in his bed. Ye'd always kiss him on his forehead. Touched him, held him, talked to him. Ye said your good-byes. And it was just the same when he took his heart attack and then a stroke. The doctor said he wouldn't last the night, but he lasted ten days and we all took turns sitting up with him. (James Kinnear)

The black plumed horses drawing the hearse in early days are etched on several memories.

But the corpse was left in the house. Then the minister would come up and say a prayer, all this sort of thing. And then perhaps the family would carry the coffin down to the hearse. It was a two black horses and a big black glass-covered hearse. It was all horses then. (John McKee)

It was only men who went to the cemetery for the actual service, usually on foot if it was to be at the old Sighthill cemetery, though Catholics would have a long journey out to St Kentigern's.

On the day of the funeral ye had the hearse. And if ye stayed near tae Sighthill Cemetery the mourners just formed in at the back of the hearse and walked along tae the cemetery. Women didnae go, it was only men. And rain, hail or shine, ye went up and stood at the cemetery with yer head doon. And ye went back to the house, those that were relatives and friends, and ye have a cup of tea and sandwiches and what have ye. (James Vaughan)

The women and children stayed inside the house, behind the drawn blinds which signalled their loss to the outside world. Other neighbours drew theirs as a sign of respect.

Funerals! Black hearse, absolutely black, and coal black horses, and plumes on! And that's going back a bit. I remember a funeral of a boy. And I can't for the life of me remember his name. But I can remember that funeral, and every curtain and every blind ... [was closed]. I mean, if it was so-and-so's death it was everybody's death. Everybody mourned. You'd never see a curtain open or a blind up. And there was a great sense of community, there really was, a great sense of community. Not that everybody got on. They didn't. But there was a great sense of community. (Margaret Burnside)

Attending funerals was important to people, but this was not always appreciated by employers outside the community.

My father told me when he was young he served his time as a printer ... Because he wasn't in the Union he couldnae get a job, so he entered the Prudential. He was in the Prudential. And his father died and they wouldnae let him stop work to go to the funeral. So he left them and got another job. (Marion Law)

After the funeral there would be tea at the house, to which neighbours would usually contribute some food.

Funerals were a worry because I don't know how much they cost, but there was always a big meal afterwards, ye know. But always at home. Nobody ever went to restaurants or any place. No, no, never. Everything was done in the house. Maybe your mother if she lived up the stair would maybe bring down ten pancakes or ten scones. And maybe somebody would bring in . . . a steak pie or a mince pie. Oh, no, it was not fancy. Everybody dressed in black. I don't know where they got it, but they dressed up in black. We never questioned it. (Mary Preece)

Catherine Richardson's mother, already a widow, lost her only other child, a daughter of nineteen, to a heart condition.

I was so very young then and I had to do things because we didn't have a father, and we didn't have many actual relatives. We had friends, but I helped my mother. I grew up very quickly because of the tragedy, ye know. And I think at that time, although I don't remember because the men went to the funeral these days, I think they still had . . . horses or something, but I don't remember, because you see I didn't see it. I was inside. They all wore black and they came back to a meal in the house.

My mother made the best of her sadness and . . . she was a wonderful mother, she didn't spoil my young life by making me miserable. She tried to be outward and things like that ye know. (Catherine Richardson)

The exclusion of women from the actual burial must often have made their grief harder to bear, as the account at the end of this book of a child's death will make clear.

10

Childbirth and Babycare

'She nursed us all. . . She actually had
ten children and one was born dead. But she
never let people feel sorry for her.'

Children normally followed a marriage within a year or so: there was almost no way of preventing it, given the lack of reliable and easily available birth control.(The first family planning clinic in Glasgow opened in 1937.) Nor was there any social reason to postpone starting a family: when women married it was almost impossible for them to continue in a job. They were expected to stay at home and have children. Only when norms were upset – in war-time, or through unemployment, or widowing – did a woman work outside the home after marriage, and then it was usually in addition to her family duties. Although it was a recurrent condition for most women, pregnancy was commonly regarded as 'not quite nice'. Like everything to do with sex, pregnancy and childbirth were attended by a remarkable amount of general reticence.

CHILDBIRTH

'Next thing, I turns roon, she's lyin' on the table.
I hears a bump. The wean lyin' on the flair!'

Childbirth was an important family event, and the value placed upon children is underlined by the very heavy expenditure, when incomes were so limited, on baby clothes. This often meant putting down instalments well in advance of an expected birth, as Mr Hoey's account of business in his family store demonstrates.

There would be much more money spent, I would think, on

children's clothing, on layettes, for example, that sort of thing, which were quite enormous. Nowadays, the list that comes from the nursing home is infinitesimal compared with the sort of lists that they had and articles of clothing which nobody even pronounces the names of now, you know, which children, small children, were put into at that time. But that was an enormous business with us and they would spend hundreds of pounds ... I mean we're talking, maybe of spending twenty pounds on something: and twenty pounds at the time we're talking about would have bought you a very good three-piece suite. (S. Graham Hoey)

38. Beautiful christening garments, c. 1920.

In a letter Mr Hoey adds: Custom had a strong hold in the area, and the prospective grandmothers on both sides would have been 'black affrontit' if the first grandchild, at least, had not been supplied with everything required. I seem to remember that the customers came equipped with some sort of an official list . . . We also sold a large number of quite expensive prams, many of which were selected many months beforehand and cash deposits paid on them every week until the baby was born.

Childbirth during this period, at least until the late 1930s, nearly always took place in the home, attended by a midwife. It was a hazardous business, as doctors were too expensive to be involved unless absolutely necessary, and mortalities from complications and post-natal infection in the days after the birth were high. (The maternal mortality figures for Glasgow were 6.3 per 1000 live births in 1915, and 7.01 in 1935; this was reduced dramatically to .33 per 1000 deliveries by 1955.) As most of these accounts show, neighbours again offered a crucial support system. Marion Smith also illustrates the secrecy which often cloaked an expected birth.

It is amazing to me when I think on it, but my mother must have done all her sewing at night. Because she made all sorts of baby clothes. But I never saw them until the baby came. I never thought on it before, but I wonder where she must have kept them!

At that time that my brother, who is the youngest of the family, . . . was born, we were all in for our lunch, the ones that were working. The ones that were at school were in too, we were all having lunch. My mother was in the room with the midwife that was handling her case, and our Peter decided to arrive at one o'clock in the day. Other babies came at queer hours of the morning, which was all right, because the children were all in bed, but Peter decided to come at one o'clock. So, the midwife just suddenly said we'd all need to get out, so the whole lot of us had to get out, and I hadn't had anything. But right up the stair, from the bottom to the top, somebody had said, 'Right, I'll take you two, I'll give them something and send them back to school, you two come in here . . . ', and so we were all given a bite to eat by the various neighbours.

[The children] all went back, ... and I went back to work.
And I must have been a kind of naive nineteen-year-old, I think I
was at that time, because one of the men in the section was
coming up the stairs and he said, 'You're late, Marion Smith, not
like you.' You know, as I was huffing and puffing up the marble
stairs. I said, 'I know, Reg, I had a wee brother at dinner time, a
baby brother at dinner time.' So I thought that was all right, I
didn't think that was funny, but they thought, you know, roaring and laughing at the idea of somebody having this in their
dinner hour! (Marion Smith)

*Joseph Cairns' story of the birth of his first child is a wonderfully
vivid narration of helplessness in the face of an event from which
men were always excluded at this period.*

Old Mrs Hawthorn, she was a midwife. And she come up one
night. I says, 'How long is this gonnae carry on here?' I waited
night after night sittin' in her Auntie Jenny's waiting on her
havin' this wean. She never had it! Then another night, same
carry-on. 'Oh, away oot' again! Now they can sit and watch it
and everything: they don't chase ye oot ...

So they said it would be two or three days before it would
happen. 'Good, good.' So the wife got up, she says 'Och, Joe, I'm
no feelin' good.' I said, 'Och, tip-toe roon the table, ye'll be as
right as a nail.' God, and I'm sittin' wi' my feet over the fire,
aboot one or two in the mornin'. Next thing, I turns roon, she's
lyin' on the table. I hears a bump. The wean lyin' on the flair!'

Me, I couldnae do nothin'. I was too shy. I was away doon like
the hammers o' heaven, doon the stairs. My mother stayed in
the bottom flat. I battered the door there and I shouted 'Ma!
Having a wean up there.' An' I run over right across the road
over tae Hawthorn. Battered her door. A nut! Wean was born ...
She [the wife] couldnae do it up the way her granny done it up,
and I couldnae do nothin'. I could do it now, I believe, but I
couldnae do it then!

*(His wife's granny was a great strong woman, idolised by Joseph,
who had in the past delivered her baby herself, cut and tied the
umbilical cord and returned to work.) Neighbours were of the
greatest importance at such times, and often did more than relatives.*

I didn't get any help from relatives, but I had a next door

neighbour who was very, very kind to me. She done ma washing for me and her daughter used to go messages for me when I was house bound, and when I did go out and take the children she used to go in and tidy up for me and see that ma dinner would be on the gas ready for me comin' back. (Isabel Miller)

My neighbour down the stair helped me when I had the boy at home. She helped me a lot. When I had the twins I had all the help I needed, and everybody was coming to the door: 'Can I take the babies out? Give me your washin'. I'll do your washin'.' The only thing is I insisted on that nobody, and I really meant it, nobody nursed them. Because they weren't in the same position as me, they couldnae nurse two, and it wasn't right to nurse one and not the other ... We used to have a couch, and I used to build up both sides of it wi' pillows and they fed themselves. 'Cause I couldnae bear to nurse one and feed it and not attend to the other one cryin'.

I met a woman about a year ago or so before the twins was born. She chapped my door the second day I came back from the hospital wi' them, and honest to God, I didnae know her. And she says to me, 'Can I help you in any way?' And I says, I don't understand her. She said, 'Can I help you with the babies?' And from that day it must have been until they went to school, that woman came right up every minute that God sent and she bathed and fed one, and I bathed and fed the other. And right up until the day she died, she still sent them a birthday card signed 'Your second mother'. An' they in turn sent her a Christmas card 'To my second mother', or a birthday card. They looked on her like that. She was a good neighbour to me in that way. And, as I say, my door was never shut. (Cathy McIlroy)

BREAST-FEEDING AND BABYCARE

'I just fed them when they gret, and if they slept past their time, I just let them.'

The first child welfare clinic were set up in Glasgow in 1906, but it was not until the early 1930s, when attendance at ante-natal clinics increased greatly, that women began to feel that experts might know better than they or their mothers or their grannies how to care for their babies. Before that babies were breast-fed when they were hungry, taken into the mother's bed, carried and cuddled often. Despite the methods practised so successfully on her ten children by Marion Smith's mother, she herself was strongly influenced by 'modern advice' and tried to keep her first daughter on a rigid feeding schedule, though she relaxed this with later children. This long narrative also illustrates the lengths people would go to before they called a doctor.

My mother had the newborn babies in the bed with her. And you can see they are coming back to that. But when I had my family, there was another way of doing it. The baby only had to be fed once in four hours. And all this kind of thing. And I was so strict about this thing. And I was doing the best, you know. And I wouldn't give her a comforter. And I wouldn't let her get sweets. And you know, then, by the time I had a second and third one I was glad to give her a comforter. I wasn't nearly so strict.

But now they're coming back to the old ways. Holding your baby like the old Glasgow women with the shawlies. Ye'd have a big tartan shawl tied round, a sort of green, and they wrapped the baby in it and wrapped the other end around and the baby was close against them and they had the warm and the comfort. Even when I was quite small, my mother had a big scarf and she would put the baby in the end of it and tuck the other end round me. I could hold this baby and it was quite safe as long as it was tucked properly in. Wrapped it round your back and tucked the right hand round the baby and brought the left hand round over the baby . . . and tucked it around at the other side.

The working class women if they were really not well-off at all, they didn't have a pram. Perambulators weren't known. Ma mother had a go-chair and the child was maybe able to sit. But she mostly carried the babies and it left her hands free . . .

She breast-fed almost all of her babies. I don't know how she managed it. But just latterly, I don't remember which baby it was, but she took an abcess in her breast. And that was an awful bad thing . . . And she was in awful agony, and one of her brothers came, and he had been in the Sanitary. He had finished some exams to be a sanitary man. He had also been in the

39. Advertisement from Hoey's, 1936.

R.E.M.C., in the army. And he had to come up to see her. And my mother's sitting like this and he had said, 'Ye'll need to get the doctor, Nan.' She had suffered so much with it, she sat and looked at a little sharp knife that she had that was a vegetable knife, and she must have been nearly crazy with the pain. She said, 'I thought if I could just maybe push this in ... ' It could have killed her nearly. It was to release this [pressure]. So he had told her what to do, and told her about hot fomentations and told her to get the doctor. She must get the doctor for that. And I don't remember the details, but she got over it.

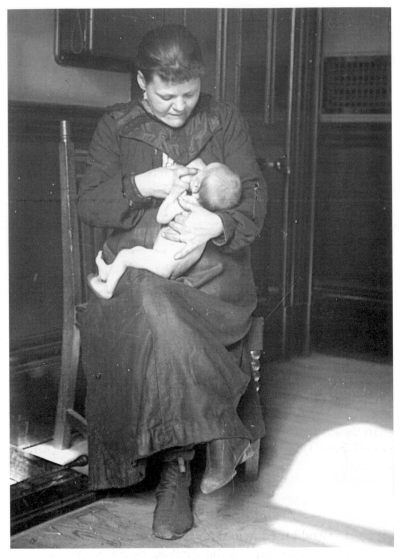

40. A mother breast-feeding her baby *c.* 1910.

She nursed us all. She was awful proud because we all had straight legs. Because people would commiserate with her, 'Oh how on earth do you manage with all those kids?' My mother would say 'Oh, quite well, they all help each other.' And she would say, 'And every one of them has straight legs.' She was always like that, my mother. She actually had ten children and one was born dead. But she never let people feel sorry for her. (Marion Smith)

Despite awareness of recommended feeding routines, Cathy Mc-Ilroy let nature decide the feeding times.

I just fed them when they gret, and if they slept past their time, I just let them. I didnae stick rigidly. No, you're no gettin' fed till four o'clock, and you're no gettin' nothing! I just fed them as I thought. I didnae overfeed them. I just – I didnae wait to the exact time. And if they were sleeping past their time I let them, I didnae wake them up in ma life to feed them. I would start about six month on the rusks as far as I could mind. I wasn't strict with them, but they didnae get away with anything, you know. I wasnae hard on them, but they knew better than to play it up to ma sort of style. (Cathy McIlroy)

The 'Green Ladies', Glasgow's visiting nurses, could be a great help, as they were to Amelia Newton, who was abandoned by her husband with eight children.

My kids were getting mince and potatoes an' they were getting fed chop bones and fat, and butterballs dipped in sugar, an' they got everything that was going. If they slept I left them sleeping, for to me a sleep was as good as a meal. They made up for it, believe you me. But at that time I was a great believer in the Green Ladies. There's nobody in the world was any greater than these Green Ladies to me. And the terrific amount of help I got off them, I mean, there was nothing I had to learn. (Amelia Newton)

FRESH AIR

'And I used to feed my children, bath them
and put them out. Lift the window, tie the pram with
the rope and tie it roon the tap in the sink.'

Fresh air was something of an obsession during this period, dating from efforts to improve public health in overcrowded urban dwellings in the second half of the nineteenth century. It was a basic ingredient in mothers' efforts to keep their families healthy, as the next chapter shows. They were well aware also of its sedating effect on babies and often took them for walks or left them outside. The ground floor window of the tenement had its advantages for this.

My children were actually put outside. As I told you, I was in the close, I was down low. And I used to feed my children, bath them and put them out. Lift the window, tie the pram with the rope and tie it roon the tap in the sink, and they were there from nine o'clock until, I would say, twelve, and they would sleep. And then they got their feed. Then the same thing happened again and again. I left them until they woke up. They were good. I was never up nor down with any of my family. (Amelia Newton)

Mrs Stronach found time to take her small children out for walks every morning and every afternoon. Children, even other neighbour's children, were important as child-minders, and altogether a lot of time was spent outside the home in childhood.

I played an awful lot with my children and I couldn't tell you all the things that we did. There was a wee field which we called the Daisy Park. And I used to walk out there with my pram and let the kids play around in the grass.

I was always out with my children. I'd walk them out in the morning and take them back at dinner time. And I'd do my big range in the morning. I'd get that done, all the rough work done. And then I'd take them up Springburn for my messages. And when they came back they would get their sleep because they were all young then. And put them down for their sleep, and I'd get my housework done, and my washing, whatever. And then we would walk out. I'd take them out always in the afternoon and bring them back at four o'clock to get dad's dinner ready.

And this wee girl that went to school, she used to come and take my oldest one out. And that took her off my hands until I got my dinner. Kept her outside playing with other children, she looked after her. I never can say that I had a bad time bringing my children up. Everything was just organized. And I always seen I got them out. I couldn't leave them with anybody and go to work all day and leave them to run about the street! (Jemima Stronach)

11

Illness, Remedies and Death

'The sanitary men came. The men burned rock sulphur on a shovel heated over the fire, and walked around wafting the fumes around the place.'

Throughout this period acute infections – scarlet fever, diphtheria, meningitis – were common, and disaster could strike a family like lightning. Chronic illness could be ruinous too. Doctors had to be paid far more than most families could afford, and were called only in extremities. As a result there are vivid memories of the home remedies used in an attempt to stave off and cure various ills without resorting to professional help. But the more serious infectious diseases were 'notifiable', and swiftly and rather severely dealt with by the authorities.

This is one aspect of the past that no one regrets. The spectacular decline in the incidence of and mortality from such diseases over the last fifty years is due to a host of public health improvements – clean water, improved sanitation, food and milk hygiene and so on – together with effective vaccines and treatments offered by a freely available health service. These accounts show how different things were within living memory.

THE COST OF ILLNESS

'Ye didnae dare get a doctor to come to your hoose.'

The death of a father, or his sickness or unemployment, could plunge the most respectable family into poverty; the death of the mother too removed an essential part of the family's precarious economic system. Hanging over all families was a very general

149

terror of the poorhouse (Barnhill) and having to 'go on the Parish'.

I hoped I'd never to go the poorhouse. In my generation, there wasn't any scivers because Tories don't give ye anything. When I was a lassie that Forresthall Hospital was called Barnhill, and my mother was terrified that we would finish up in the poorhouse. Terrified! Now when we were kids, we used to come and play doon there and look at Forresthall. An' I used to say to my pa, 'I hope I never go to the poorhouse.' That's the way ye were brought up. Ye were terrified! That's your Victorian values! The poorhouse! But it showed you that there was people that cared for the poor. I had an uncle that was idle at that time, the great depression. And he'd five kids. And he stayed in Anderston. And if he didnae walk from Anderston to Forresthall or Barnhill to chop wood, his kids, he didnae get a penny tae feed them! And it didnae matter whether it was rain, hail or snow. He had to walk from Anderston to Barnhill, chop wood all day, walk back! I think ma mother said he got five shilling a week. But if he didnae go, if he wis sick and he couldnae go to chop that wood, nothing! They kids got nothing. Oor kids! My generation! . . .

Aye, there were a lotta doctors. But then ye didnae dare get a doctor to come to your hoose. 'Cause very few folk could afford to have a house call. They couldnae afford to pay a doctor to come unless, as I say, it was an urgent thing. But any minor childhood thing your mother doctored you and that was it. But there was nothing to help you if your mother hadnae the money. Forget it. Ye wirnae getting any. (Betty Knox)

A family with a little spare money could insure after a fashion by joining one of the many self-help friendly societies which were an important buffer against sudden destitution.

If you called in the doctor it cost you two and sixpence for his visit, then you had to buy the medicine. But most people were in societies and they paid the bills. Our family was in the Ancient Shepherds who met in the Masonic Hall in Vulcan St. (Sam Watt)

Marion Smith remembers the perils of childbirth for her mother and the general worries of bringing up children in this period. Her memories explain clearly why many people, of her generation especially, feel so strongly about the National Health Service instituted in 1948. In the light of recent changes in funding and the increasing

*numbers joining 'societies' like BUPA for private insurance against
medical costs, some might feel that the wheel is now turning full
circle.*

Imagine what that [the National Health Service] would have
meant to my mother. And the benefit of being able to space your
family. Family limitation. She wouldn't have had to have nine
children. In the circumstances, there was no way of avoiding it.
You just had to take the children as they all came. And never
once in hospital! Several times she was very close to death
because she had severe haemorrhages, and there was no blood
transfusions as there is today, which would have picked her up.
And she had to lie in the bed there and we were all having our
meals and our life going on all round about her. It wasn't
peaceful for her. Different children climbing up on her bed to say,
'Could you do this, could you do that?'

It seems remarkable to me looking back in the light of today,
that my mother with her nine children and father's pitifully low
wage had to pay for everything. Ye had tae pay for the doctor
every time he came. With the result that my mother was a fund
of knowledge without needing a doctor, unless it was something
of an infectious nature which had to be reported. And you had to
pay the doctor right on the nail. (Marion Smith)

MOTHER'S REMEDIES

She made up each winter her own emulsion from a
recipe. It had cod liver oil in it. But it was condensed milk . . .
She made up this in a big lemonade bottle.'

*Fresh air, as we have already seen, was held quite rightly to be a
powerful preventative of ill-health. It was also for many the first
recourse for a cure. There was firm belief in the efficacy of the 'seven
winds' that passed across the highest point of Springburn; and in the
light of today's research on negative and positive ionization and the
bad or beneficial effects of certain winds, it is seems that this might
have been more than superstition.*

Dae ye know when we were young, I think it was two
shillings if ye had tae go to a doctor. We were poor. My mother, if

ye said, 'I've got a sore throat', Ma would say, 'Away oot and play. Let the wind get at you.' Because she was terrified that ye'd need to go to a doctor. And that was how ye were brought up, because you had nothing!

My mother used to say that up at Carlisle Street there was seven winds that used to circulate the air. And my mother used to say to us when we were kids, 'Go up and sit in the bowling green.' And we used to go because we thought that the seven winds made ye healthy. (Betty Knox)

41. The bowling green on Keppochhill Road where Springburn's seven healthy winds blew.

She used to say, 'Let the air get at it', because it was the quickest way of healing. If ye had a sore thing. My mother had always declared that. She always said that about her babies. She never had any of them with nappy rash. Because she would let them lie out on the top of a cot blanket or something for just a wee while just to let the air get at them. That was the thing then. (Marion Smith)

The ever-present pot of home-made soup had a good deal of nourishment in it, so that most families of this class started with a reasonable diet; and an ailing child could usually be coaxed into sipping at least the broth from the soup. Simple medicaments were often disguised as sweets which made them very popular: Amelia Newton's mother put mustard powder in her homemade toffee for colds. It is now known that deficiencies of certain vitamins and trace elements increase susceptibility to infection, so home-made tonics like Mrs Russell's cod liver oil mixture, rich in vitamins A and D, certainly had some protective value.

She had the old-fashioned sort of remedies. She made up each winter her own emulsion from a recipe and it tasted far nicer than the ordinary one. And we all took it. And it had cod liver oil in it. But it was made with condensed milk. It made it sort of sweet. But we got the cod liver oil and she made up this in a big lemonade bottle. She also seemed to know all they things. She would send us down to the chemist. I always remember, Ipece-chuana wine. It was an expectorant when you had a cough. Syrup of squills [also an expectorant]. I know that if we had a wee sort of kidney infection or chill on the kidneys – I think it was sweet spirits of nitre.

Of course for chest things, it was always camphorated oil. And there was a stuff called Thermogene. Well, it was a sort of orange or pinky-coloured cottonwool. They sold it in a roll. And it was impregnated with something that was good for your chest, you know. They put this on the wee ones. Back and front with a slit for the head to go through. Put it on like a wee waistcoat thing back and front. And you wore that next to your skin. 'Cause the heat drew out whatever it was from whatever impregnated the wadding. You had to wear it all winter. You took it off and it got washed, but back on went your wee waistcoat. Then when it came to the spring and you were doing away with this, you had to take if off, according to my mother, a piece at a time so that you didn't lose all the benefit at once. We got lesser and less. We took a little piece off every day. .... It did have a kind of a smell. When ye put it on, it heated up with your body throughout.

You could get off of the chemist camphorated crystals and put it in a locket. That was quite nice. You wore it round your neck and it had wee holes in it and the camphorated stuff came out and it helped your chest too. But camphorated oil, my mother did rub us with it if you had a very bad cold.

She used to heat salt and put it in a sock. Tie the end of the sock, and fix it round your throat for a sore throat. My eldest daughter was laughing the other day when I was mentioning it.

42. Marion Smith's mother, Mrs Russell, standing, with
her Aunt Sarah, *c.* 1905.

She said 'Oh Mum', she said, 'the other day it came to my mind you saying that about Grandma', and she said, 'I did that too for a sore throat, and it worked!' And I think why it's a sock, it's a handy thing you have and it sort o' fitted round your throat. It retained the heat. My mother also had a thing for sore throats, a treatment that she said was Dr Kirk's treatment. Now who Dr Kirk was I do not know. It was a cold cloth, cold water, run under cold water, and put next to your sore throat. And then another dry thing put on the top, and gradually, the cold compress drew out the heat from the sore throat, and it became hot again. But you used to think 'I cannae think to put cold water on your sore throat.' But it worked! (Marion Smith)

Joseph Cairns remembers the infamous home blood cleanser, sulphur and treacle, known as brimstone and treacle in some parts.

The only illness I mind o' was somethin' to do with boils. The doctor came to ye and he went, 'Oh, I don't know!' Big boils. An' that was all over your system. At one time people were great ones for givin' ye [home] medicines. Supposed to help ye. It's sulphur and treacle. And ye took this and that wis supposed tae help ye. Christ! It brought ye oot in boils. Och! (Joseph Cairns)

INFECTIOUS DISEASE

'When you saw the green van coming you knew it was Ruchill. You knew it was scarlet fever.'

Infectious diseases for which there was little effective treatment still swept through the population in the early days of this period. Smallpox has now been eradicated from the world but was endemic in Britain early in this century. The effect of an epidemic could be catastrophic as this account shows, leaving families entirely dependent upon neighbours.

There was the time there was the smallpox scare in Springburn, that was after the war, the First World War. The soldiers were all coming back. The Spanish Flu they called it. And I always remember my mother saying that there wasn't a close that didn't have something. It was an epidemic. There's a girl, she still goes about Springburn, and her face still has the spot marks. She was one of the lucky ones, because they were dying off like flies because they didn't have vaccination at that time.

But there was a particular family that lived in our close and they were Irish and the boys used to play with my brothers. Well, the father came back [from the war] and his wife was expecting another baby, and she took this Spanish Flu. The father died and the mother died. Now they were left with all the family. They weren't even teenagers. And at that time my mother and this other neighbour Mrs Pate, they used to make pots of soup to keep the family together until someone came over from Ireland. But my mother used to make pots of soup and leave it to them because it was a good wee while before someone came over. (Jean Hanton)

Betty Knox recalls from the 1920s the unsanitary conditions of some of the play areas which she feels were a source of infection. Her theory of natural 'immunization' may well have some truth in it: many children exposed to tuberculosis developed immunity with minimal clinical symptoms, and the same thing is seen where viral hepatitis is endemic.

There used to be scarlet fever, diphtheria. These diseases were rife. When we were kids, whole families o' kids got taken away, because the middens were all open middens. Ye used to shout up for a piece. Your mother threw ye a piece intae the backcourt. Ye'd be playin' wi' a ball. It maybe jumped intae the midden. You jumped in. You were black. And I think we were immunized! I fortunately never had anything like that when I wis young. But many, many children roon about where we lived died with diphtheria. And many more had scarlet fever! (Betty Knox)

In fact whooping cough and measles, which are now notifiable, accounted for more deaths in Glasgow as a whole than either of these diseases. The mortality figures for children under ten for 1910-1914 expressed per million are: scarlet fever 721, diphtheria and croup 993, whooping cough 2535, and measles 2558. Improvements in public health in the 1930s are reflected in the comparable figures for 1935-39: scarlet fever 108, diphtheria and croup 715, whooping cough 959 and measles 630. Scarlet fever is not now a serious disease; in the past there were frequent complications, like acute rheumatic fever, which caused damage to the heart. Diphtheria

*was conquered by an intensive immunisation programme intro-
duced in 1940. (In Glasgow in 1955 there were no deaths from
scarlet fever, diphtheria or whooping cough, and only 25 from
measles.) In pre-war years scarlet fever and diphtheria had to be
reported to the Sanitary Department which made attempts to disin-
fect houses, and curtail their spread, as Marion Smith remembers of
the 1920s.*

There was, mind you, a great deal of infection about in these
days. Milk was kept in shops in open containers. At times there
was an epidemic which spread like wild fire. At one time four of
us were in Ruchill Hospital with scarlet fever. One of my sisters
had diphtheria, and although ultimately she recovered, she had
a heart condition for the rest of her days and died early.

Measles and whooping cough were treated at home, but
scarlet fever and diphtheria were 'notifiable' and you went to the
hospital. The sanitary men came and took particulars and tried
to pinpoint the source of the epidemic. They also came to disin-
fect the house. We had to evacuate the house and my mother
had to walk around for over an hour with the children while the
men burned rock sulphur on a shovel heated over the fire, and
walked around wafting the sulphur fumes around the place. I
doubt if this was effective, but that's what was done.

You also were entitled to a free washing which was a great
benefit as all the clothes came back from the Corporation wash-
houses clean and dry. On the day you were to get this washing
done there was always some neighbour or other came asking
you to include a large bedmat or quilt or a pair of blankets in your
bundle. The men who collected the washing had to expostulate,
'Oh Missus, is this all yours?' My mother, of course, could blandly
reply, 'Do you know how many children I have?' (Marion Smith)

*The arrival of the green van from the Sanitary Department was
the signal to the neighbourhood that someone was going to be taken
to the hospital with an infectious disease, or was having their house
disinfected for various other problems.*

You had the green van where it came up tae the house. That
was your Health [Sanitary Department]. And the green van,
when ye had bugs, and all the kids wet the beds, and the
neighbours complained. And then the green van came up, took

everything and fumigated it. The house and everything, ye know! And in the close, 'Whisper, whisper'! (Alec McGregor)

Head lice were endemic, as they still are in British schools. Mothers combatted them with coal tar soap, careful combing and dire warnings to their children not to go too near dirty neighbours. If the authorities were called to deal with the problem the methods almost deliberately marked the children with the stigma of infection: shaved heads meant lice; a purple-stained skin signified impetigo or scabies – both of which are still quite common though there are better and less obvious treatments for them today.

Impetigo! That was your Gentian Violet. Oh, God. Ye know, ye couldnae even go to school. Ye used to get the Gentian ... round the back, ye know, and the nose. They didnae care in these days. Like if ye hid lice. Ye knew the bloke had lice, because his head was completely shaven, and there were a can-can [a fringe of hair]. A can-can! They were a wee bit liberal. They left ye with a can-can at the front, hair parted! But it wis only aboot half an inch broad an' the rest o' yer head wis shaved. And yer oxters [underarms] were shaved. (Alec McGregor)

HOSPITALS

'It's weeks and weeks, and days and days,
since I've seen my home.
Father, mother, take me away
from this convalescent home.'

Jean Parker remembers the green van the day she was taken away with scarlet fever. She was kept in hospital for nine months, during which time she only saw her mother once. Her surprising conclusion that she quite enjoyed being in hospital was mostly to do with being let off school for the period!

They've eradicated a lot of these diseases, such as scarlet fever. There used to be a lot of that during the summer holidays. I remember standing waiting till the ambulance came. You used to say, 'Do you know who's going away in the ambulance?' And everyone would gather round to see who it was [laugh]! And when you saw the green van coming you knew it was Ruchill.

You knew it was scarlet fever. And they kept you in for six weeks. And they used to shave your head and everything. They said you sweat so much. By the time I went they must have had advanced a bit cause they never cut my hair or anything.

I remember not being very well one night, I had a sore eye. My eye was all swollen ... And ma mother thought actually I'd got a draught, because it wis all black. And she sent for the doctor. And within an hour I was in Ruchill! I couldn't see out this eye for about two months. Once they got the poison all drained out I was beginning to get my sight back. But they kept me in because they couldn't get the fever to come down. I had still a temperature and, och, I just wisnae well. But once I got over that I was fine.

I was very ill during Christmas an' that. I never got ma presents till I came home in April. I never saw my mother or father from August till Christmas eve. They weren't allowed to come in. And then on Christmas eve everybody was asleep. I was twelve and I was the oldest in the ward and everybody was sleeping. They woke me up and my mother was standing at the bedside. She had on a big white robe with a thing round her mouth, and the hat on. She never saw me again till I came out in April, that was me. I was nearly nine months in Ruchill Hospital.

Anything that had been given as presents in the hospital at Christmas I wasn't allowed to bring home. So my mother and father had left all my presents till I came home. So that was great. I quite enjoyed being in the hospital. (Jean Parker)

Quarantining in hospital was an attempt to restrict the spread of the diseases: it did not greatly assist recovery. The complete exclusion of parents reveals the frequently overbearing but scarcely questioned measures of the authorities – the psychological trauma involved was not considered. The hospitalisation of Cathy Craig seemed unbearably inhumane to her father: he removed her and cured her eventually with 'fresh air'.

I had diphtheria. I was five years of age. And my mother and father couldnae get to see me. It was just through the glass. With a wee white gown on, my head shaved. So my father said, 'Right, that's it. She's no gettin' any pity from anybody.' Took us oot and the doctor says, 'Do you realize what'll happen to you if anything happens to your child in your care. You are held responsible.' He says, 'Aye!' Hurled me about in a pram till I got better. It was aboot a year till I got better. And that was the kind a hospital it was, it was very old-fashioned.

The psychological resilience of children is often remarkable. Taking it all in their stride, tenement children had skipping-rope games in which they would sing rhymes about Ruchill Hospital. Betty Smith after all the years remembers them well.

> It's weeks and weeks, and days and days,
> since I've seen my home.
> Father, mother, take me away
> from this convalescent home.

> Here comes the doctor, Doctor McRay
> To see his patient, every second day,
> Are you better? Are you worse?
> Clap your hands and kiss your nurse.

> Here comes the nurse with the red-hot poultice,
> Claps it on and takes no notice.
> Oh, says the patient, that's too hot,
> Oh, says the nurse, that is not.

> I'm going home on Monday morning.
> I'm going home at ten o'clock.
> Good-bye doctors, good-bye sisters,
> Good-bye, good-bye to all the nurses.

> Farewell to the nurses of Ruchill,
> Farewell to the Ruchill home.
> Farewell to the doctors and sisters,
> But nurses are best of them all.

> Oh, nursie, oh nursie, oh nursie dear,
> I'll think of your troubles when I'm far from here.
> When your troubles are all over I'll come back again,
> Back to dear old Ruchill to see the nurses again.
> Some hopes!! (Skipping song)

Consumption, the popular name for pulmonary tuberculosis which 'consumed' the body, was another major killer; indeed until the Second World War Glasgow had the highest death-rate in the

43. Staff at Stobhill Hospital Springburn, during the
First World War.

country from tuberculosis. The Scots and Irish are among the races
particularly susceptible to this disease, which has now been con-
trolled through milk pasteurization, vaccines and effective anti-
biotics.

See that consumption, it was actually worse than AIDS. That
were more folk died in a week in Glasgow! Like ye had no
chance. I lost aboot five blokes and aboot seven lassies to
consumption. They went tae Robroyston and Ruchill. The privileged went tae Switzerland. If ye couldnae get into Ruchill or
Robroyston you were dead. They used to steam blankets, ye
know, and put them over ye.

Funnily enough, the hair was beautiful and ye had the pink
complexion. The lassies looked beautiful, really, as if they were
made up. But they were like wax dummies. Ye got the galloping
consumption . . . six weeks and you were dead. Out of a hundred
people that had consumption only three lived.

Even a worse thing in kids was diphtheria. This is what I
cannae understand . . . The brain disease. Well, all the wives and
my mother would say, 'Now don't go near him! He's got
meningitis.' (Alec McGregor)

THE DEATH OF A CHILD

'We had a wee one, a beautiful child she was, who died.'

Death, like birth, commonly took place in the home. It might seem, looking back, that in families usually much larger than today's, families that lived daily with the knowledge that illness could easily be fatal, that the relatively common experience of losing a child would be easier to accept. But while a few people talked with apparent detachment about such family losses, it was often clear that this was far from the case: the pain is still there after all these years. The importance of helping bereaved siblings has probably only been recognised over the last twenty years or so. In the past they were often sent away and left to cope with their grief alone.

Marion Smith's love for her eight sisters and one brother, and her involvement in the raising of 'our children', have been amply attested in these pages. When she was twelve her little sister Grace, aged two-and-a-half, died of meningitis. She was deeply affected, and found it hard to be excluded from the funeral. Her mother too suffered a profound depression for which, as Marion says, she would certainly have been treated today. There can be few more moving accounts of such devastating bereavement in a tenement family.

I was really older than my years. That's why fairy tales were such an escape for me. We had one wee one, a beautiful child she was, who died. She had meningitis and there was nothing they could do for her. Grace was two and a half when she died, a long drawn out [illness]. I was sitting up, my mother was sitting up. We were all sitting up. Dad, my mother and myself, when Dad was there, because she was lying in the kitchen [on the recess bed]. But she died.

... She was left in the other room along with us children in her wee white coffin. Because we just had the two rooms. And you're cooking and having all your meals in the other room. But we weren't frightened or anything. To us, she was beautiful because she was ours. She was like a little doll, and she was in this beautiful wee white coffin. And I remember my mother put a wee lace bonnet on her. And my mother put socks on her feet sayin' 'She'll be cold.'

It was only when I grew up and I remembered it that I thought 'How awful'. I was told to go away for the funeral. And I had felt that I had really had a sort of interest. She was as much my baby as my mother's. I was told, 'Take the children and go away. You're all to go away and go to Aunt Mary's in Station Road.' But I resented being sent away. Well, I did what I was told, but I didn't go very far. I went and stood in Arthur's close. That's Mrs Arthur's close, right next to the Princes. Stood with the children there. Because I wanted to see what they were going to do with Grace. I don't know what was in my mind. The coffin was just sitting in one of the cabs [horse drawn]. I just saw them going away, and I felt, 'Well, that's it and there's nothing you can do about it.' Then I took the children away up to my Aunt Mary's.

My mother never knew to this day that I had stayed to see . . . Because I remember sitting waiting up with Grace all through the night, well just waiting with her. But she wasn't moving or doing anything, and they'd sent me out the next day, through the day, for a message up to the Co-operative or something. Sent me out, and when I came back, Grace had died. And I thought, and felt, that if I had been there, I wouldn't have let it happen. And there is no way I could have. I really thought, 'They sent me out. They sent me away.' I thought, 'If I had been there, I wouldn't have let her go.' It shows you. They don't think that children are affected much by that.

But after that, another family came to stay in the other house in the close, and they had a wee one, very fair like our Grace, silky fair hair. And they were from Ireland. And I got a wee stool, and sat in the close and nursed that wee one. And it helped me. She was small and fair, and just about the same age. And I felt but for that, I would have felt very bad indeed. I was depressed, yes.

I went back to school at that time up at higher grade, and I had a teacher who was very, very good with me. She never knew I had been sitting up with Grace for a good wee while, and I wasn't getting my sleep. And this day, this Miss Morrison came up and she said I don't know what has gone wrong with you Marion, your work has gone bad . . . what on earth's wrong with you?' I put my head down on the desk. And cried. It was the best thing that could have happened to me. I told her, because she hadn't known anything about it.

It stayed with me a long time. Because, one of my sisters had been making up a family tree. For a cousin in Canada ... I looked it over, and I said 'You haven't put Grace in.' They had all come after Grace. They didn't even know about her. And I put her name in. The younger members of the family had no idea about Grace. But Mary and myself and the next sister, we all knew Grace. From time to time, my mother would say 'Grace would have been' and she would say what age she would have been.

My mother was so ... she just sat. Sat and didn't move. And she had a doll, a very pretty doll that Grace had been given as a present. And she sat with this doll on her knees. And by today's [standards] they would have done something for my mother. It was the deepest, most deep depression. And they didn't do a thing.

All they said was, the best thing that could happen was another child. Well it happened that my mother had Nancy. And she absolutely lavished ... She made baby clothes, my mother. She was a great sewer. She made beautiful baby clothes for Nancy. She was far, far better dressed than any of us. And my mother, she had a bright cashmere shawl with silk fringes and silk embroidery. And at that time they wore veils. She had a veil, a fine net veil and a big white satin bonnet. Oh, she went over the top with our Nancy! That helped. It really helped. She had another baby to nurse. My mother was mad about babies. She had her the year after. And it really helped all of us. (Marion Smith)

Epilogue: Then and Now

'Well, I'm not the first person to say this.
Lots of people say that the sense of closeness
in the tenements was something.'

These pages of oral history, full of human warmth and vitality, have given a strong sense of the patterns of daily existence in a cohesive tenement community where relatives lived close and neighbours were good. It is overall a very positive picture: some of the interviewees themselves are aware of a tendency to idealise 'the good old days'.

The only danger in all this is that you, as an outsider, begin to think that [Springburn] must have been the garden of Eden. But it wasn't. You had the well-to-do, you had the drunks and all the rest of it, you had the various mistakes of society ... But you see, it was a good working-class district, because we were all tradesmen. (Bobby McGee)

This record of what people found valuable in lives which otherwise had little material comfort has much to teach us today about the building of strong communities. The tenements may have been unfit to live in by modern standards, but as a building type they were very well adapted to communal life. The background to the sweeping away of the old tenements in many parts of Glasgow, and the sense of loss experienced by those who grew up in them, was outlined in the introduction. While the destruction of the tenement way of life is entangled with much greater, irrevocable changes affecting all sectors of society – chiefly the conversion of people into consumers, and the centralising of the provision of all sorts of needs – the comments of people who remember it and have seen their lives change so much since the Second World War are worth listening to.

Our technocratic age, at a time when many state supports are being withdrawn or reduced, can profit from the experience and wisdom of a caring community with a great range of survival skills.

Some lessons indeed have already been learned. Architects and planners are beginning to listen to the requests of people who will live in new buildings. Neighbourliness and co-operativeness are at last being tapped, through the formation of tenants' associations and housing co-operatives, with very positive results even in some of the unmanageable peripheral housing estates which are Glasgow's present problem. As for the tenements themselves, wholesale demolition has stopped. Now stone-cleaned and refurbished these solid buildings have come back into their own.

Willie Dewar introduces these extracts, reeling off many of the common accusations against the way things are now, expressing a feeling of hurt and helplessness in the face of the major developments imposed from outside.

There was pride taken all over Springburn. All working-class people, all good class of people, working-class people. They could have saved a terrible lot of houses in Springburn. They should have never been allowed to put roads the way they done. These roads weren't necessary 'cause you've still got a build up of traffic yet. With the same money they could have built houses. They could have modernized [the tenements] up and people would have stayed here yet, instead of scattering all over the place.

The people kept them good and clean. The toilets were spotless and everything. It was all working-class people and they kept their toilets, they kept their stairs clean. Good communicators! They spoke to one another. Now they're living in these big flats, nobody speaks to one another, just passing one another by.

There's not a place where kids could go, no picture house, nothing, everything's been taken away. I think the way they've modernized things has made the place worse. 'Cause I think there should be a couple of picture houses for the kiddies to go tae and keep them off their mothers' backs, the way it was years ago. There wasnae so much vandalism. There's no pictures noo. It was cheaper then, tuppence, ye know, matinees.

There was crime, but not a lot, the crime rate was very low. Years ago people were happy. They were all working-class people in Springburn, nice people. Ye could walk out and leave yer door open: you couldn't dare leave your door open nowadays. They weren't interfering wi' the like of old people or that. There was nae mugging old women or that in these days. That seems to be the crime nowadays, mugging the old people. (William Dewar)

Others see pragmatically that employment is the key. Sam Watt, for instance, who no longer lives in Springburn but frequently visits, feels that the modern houses are all right, but what the community needs is to 'get some modern factories and bring back some good old-fashioned employment'. Springburn grew up as a community built round its work-places. Men could easily come home for their midday meal. Now there is 27% unemployment, and those that do work are mostly commuters to other places. Work no longer underpins and enhances the cohesivness of the community.

Well to me the only improvement could have come if employment had continued in Springburn. I mean it was when the employment was going away from Springburn, that's really when the heart was going out of Springburn. Part of it has been with ... a policy that they were going to reduce the number of people ... and they were going to shove them into over-spill areas, East Kilbride, Kirkintilloch, so forth. Now this was all encouraged at the first, the people went out, ... the condition of the houses and so forth were allowed to go down. Then when the works started to leave the area that's when the area really started to deteriorate, because nothing was coming back in. It was only later that they didnae realise that instead of tearing down a lot of the tenements they could refurbish the tenements that there were. (Sam Watt)

People have no hankering to go back to the grim living conditions of the tenement houses as they were. They are ready to acknowledge that the new multi-storey flats and housing schemes offered greatly improved facilities: more room, running hot water, bathrooms. The original delight of rehousing is nicely expressed here.

We went up tae the Milton, and we used tae shout, 'Yoo-hoo' tae everybody. 'Yoo-hoo, I'm in the end room.' 'Yoo-hoo I'm in the boys' room.' 'Yoo-hoo I'm in the kitchen.' Ye know, ye could hardly find each other! Whereas in Balgray Hill ye were trippin' over each other. Now today they say these houses [in the schemes] are rotten, they're terrible. (Robert Lister)

The social consequences of rehousing old communities in hi-rise flats took some time to emerge. Criticism often mentions their unsuitability, compared with the tenements, for raising children.

Well at the time [the hi-rise flats] were going up I must say we didn't see the wrongs of it then. I mean the housing situation being as it was, this seemed marvellous, you know. But it wasn't till they were up that all the various faults began to show up, that they weren't handy for kids. It's not the type of building to keep a family in, I mean if you're twenty storeys up and wee Johnny's down below then you cannae really keep an eye on them. They didn't create at that time proper amenities such as play-grounds and things like that for the flats that they could use for the kids or even proper facilities at that time, they just stuck the flats up and got people in. At the time they were O.K.: it was great housing as compared with what they were in and there was a great need for housing, but I'm afraid that we've since it was a bit of a disaster. (Peter Russell)

44. Old tenements coming down *c.* 1970, with maisonettes behind, in Springburn Road, Balgray Hill.

*Marion Smith acknowledges the benefits of the Welfare State –
though in fact this centralised provision of the needs which had once
perforce been met from the community is a significant contributor to
the breakdown of the networks of neighbourliness which this book
records. She focuses on the loss of the sense of community which
was the price for rehousing, and identifies as important the destruction of the old controls over the safety and behaviour of children.*

And for today, the benefits are the Health Service. Because, in
those days everything had to be paid for. And when you were
out of work, you got no pay for this as they do now. There were
no unemployment benefits ... And every pen, book, jotter, pen-
cil, thimble for your sewing class, you had to pay for all of it. In
the main though there are more benefits [nowadays].

But the good things about long ago was for children in
playing, because nowadays there is the increased traffic. The
community of children from the tenements were able to be out
on the street without having to be watched out for, motor cars
and things like that. We could play in Gourlay Street with very
little trouble. We had full games of rounders and all sorts of
things like that with a whole crowd of children playing together.

The community spirit of the tenement, the neighbourliness,
was a thing that has been lost. Because people got better houses,
but they were all out in schemes. Whole communities were
broken up that had lived together in the tenements for years.
Everybody knew everybody else. And as I have said before children sort of belonged to the community. They were better
behaved because every neighbour took to do with you, because if
they saw you misbehaving or doing something wrong or climbing on the wash-houses everybody would say, 'I'll tell your
mother. Come down out of there.' You belonged to your three
closes, or whatever. Everybody had to do with you, and you
didn't get up to so many things. And people were more tolerant
of children then. You were the community's children. (Marion
Smith)

*The tenements had been directly integrated with a wide variety of
shops, and Springburn itself, like similar communities, was busy
and self-sufficient. The sense of imprisonment in the new estates
soon became intense.*

They made a mistake, they built houses, nothing but houses: they forgot about shops and cinemas and pubs. Now that meant that when you moved up to Balornock you were a prisoner in Balornock, there was nothing round about. If you went up that street and down that street you were just seeing a replica of the street you lived in. There was half dozen shops ... and there were no cinemas. People used to say it was a week's wages for travelling, you know, because you had further to come by bus. (Bobby McGee)

Ah, well that's sad. When I think of what it was in my days: Springburn was really like a small town. You didn't need to go into the town as we talk about it, you know into the city centre in Glasgow, to get anything. You had a large emporium like Hoey's: you could get [everything] you needed there from a needle to an anchor. You were well served, as you see, with cinemas and dance-halls with all sorts of social activities going on. (Peter Russell)

Of course it is the deep changes wrought by the growth of the post-war consumer society – by motor-cars and shopping-centres; television and home-videos – which have done away with the shops and the cinemas and dance-halls. The old-fashioned shopping is repeatedly mourned as another expression of the 'we-feeling' of tenement life, which has been replaced by a sense of alienation in the face of the anonymity of modern urban existence.

The old tenements had a character to them. The wee shops! Every shopkeeper practically knew ye. They knew ye fae ye were local. And ye went in, and they knew ye ... It had that wee one to one. You got service. But you go into a big supermarket, you don't even get civility, never mind service. Naebody wants tae know ye. They just want the money at the till. That's no' a nice world! (Betty Knox)

The security of the past has been replaced by a widespread fear of the outside world today.

We could walk about the streets without any fear or favour. The hardest thing that came up the street was the coal-cart. (James Vaughan)

Nobody ever said worse than ma name. I've come from the dancin', and walked the roads as well. Ye never heard o' muggin'. I've walked fae here over tae Springburn Park, one o'clock in the mornin', four o'clock in the mornin', twelve o'clock at night. (Agnes Muirhead)

More than anything else it is this friendliness and sense of belonging that is missed, the neighbourliness which was essential and natural in a community reliant upon itself for the provision of so many of its needs – for mutual support in hard times and for socializing in an unmaterialistic society.

I was saddened at the look of Springburn now. It was such a grand place to live in, to be brought up in, in the old days. It was thriving, busy. Things were good for the men, they were in work, all in the works. There were also the times, of course, when there wasn't any work. But in the main people all knew one another. We used to go on holiday. The only holidays ever we would go on were to my grandma's. She had a house in Millport, for letting, and we used to go down there. And we'd go down and on the road my mother would say, 'Oh, that's a Springburn face', and what she meant was it's someone that she knew, by seeing, just going about Springburn. She didn't know their name or anything, but she knew it was a Springburn face.

I mean maybe it was all for the best but I don't think so. I mean there was a feeling about Springburn. Everybody seemed to be very friendly with everybody else in Springburn, but you don't get it nowadays at all. (Peter Russell)

There have of course been many improvements in the lives of individuals, as Peter Russell notes.

I can definitely see that . . . I had a better life than my father had, well from what I can remember about his life . . . I think that I progressed into a better home life, better conditions and things like that. And my sons I think have had a slightly better education than myself and better opportunities. (Peter Russell)

But his sister Marion Smith speaks for many when she sums up:

Well, I'm not the first person to say this. Lots of people say that the sense of closeness in the tenements was something. People moved out to different areas, families were broken up, the aunts and uncles no longer just stay near. Improved conditions certainly, but something has been lost. (Marion Smith)

Once the community had established itself, it absorbed new

immigrants, from Ireland and rural Scotland, very easily, accommodating differences in religion and class without problems. It was a
stable community, with a strong sense of continuity.

Marion Smith at her baby sister's funeral in 1919 hid in
Arthur's Close, the close between 42 Gourlay Street and the Princes
Picture House. Her brother Peter Russell remembers being chased
out of in this same close by Mrs Arthur in 1934. This author who
lived in the same close as the Russells had done so many years
before, played in Arthur's close with a favourite friend, Catherine
Arthur, in the 1950s. There was tradition in our closes, and there
was family history. The upper classes lived for generations in their
mansions, but we lived for generations 'up oor closes'.

Perhaps it is fitting to end with this statement from John
Wotherspoon, which reflects the search for elements of continuity in
a time of rapid change which underlies much current nostalgia:

If Springburn developed and there was an opportunity I'd like
to go back there. Your roots are where you were born. It'll never
be the same, Springburn, but I'd like to go back there.

45. Gourlay Street c. 1960. The close where the Russells and the
author lived is the first beyond the shop; Arthur's close is the next.
Only the little Gourlay St School building, far left, remains today.

Glossary

back	*back court or green: an enclosed area behind a tenement block used for drying clothes etc.*
ben the room	*through in the other room.*
bunnet	*man's cap*
chap the door	*knock on the door*
close	*shared entry passage to a tenement block*
dyke	*wall*
fae	*from, from the fact that*
flit	*move from a house*
girdle	*griddle - a flat iron plate for baking*
go-cart	*a hand-pushed cart*
go-chair	*push-chair*
greet	*cry*
house	*often used where standard English would say 'flat'*
how	*why*
hurly-bed	*a bed on wheels*
idle	*often means unemployed*
lum	*chimney*
messages	*shopping*
midden	*three-sided rubbish area in a back court*
mind	*remember*
piece	*piece of bread or sandwich*
the room	*the parlour/bedroom in a 'room-and-kitchen' house*
semmit	*undershirt*
shot	*a turn at something*
single-end	*a one-room house*
stay	*live*
steamie	*the public wash-house*
steep	*to soak (clothes etc)*
totie	*tiny*
wally	*made of china, glazed earthenware*
wean	*child*

Select Bibliography

Checkland, S. G., *The Upas Tree: Glasgow 1875-1975* (Glasgow 1976)

Cunnison, J., and Gilfillan, J. B. S., eds, *The Third Statistical Account of Scotland: Glasgow* (Glasgow 1958)

Hutchison, Gerard and O'Neill, Mark, *The Springburn Experience: An Oral History of Work in a Railway Community from 1840 to the Present Day* (Edinburgh 1989)

Jacobs, Jane, The Death and Life of the Great American Cities: The Failure of Town Planning (New York 1961)

McIlvanney, William, *Shades of Grey: Glasgow 1956-1987* (Edinburgh 1989)

Nicolson, Murdoch, and O'Neill, Mark, *Glasgow, Locomotive Builder to the World* (Edinburgh 1987)

Smout, T. C., *A Century of the Scottish People, 1830-1950* (London 1986)

Thompson, Paul, *The Voice of the Past: Oral History* (Oxford 1986)

Worsdall, Frank, *The Glasgow Tenement: A Way of Life* (1979; 2nd edn Glasgow 1989)

Young, M., and Willmott, P., *Family and Kinship in East London* (London 1955)

Index

Italicised numbers refer to illustrations.

Illustration Acknowledgements

For permission to reproduce illustrations we thank: Springburn Museum, 2, 6 & 7 (photo John Thomas), 12, 14 (photo John Thomas), 17, 21, 24-37, 38 (photo M. Graham), 41, 43, 44 (photo Ken Wilcox), 45 (photo John Thomas); J. Halley, 22; Mr S. Graham Hoey, 8, 13, 16, 39; the Lister family, 1, 9, 10, 20, 23; the Mitchell Library, Glasgow 15, 29 (Graham Collection); Peter Russell, 42; Strathclyde Regional Archives 4, 5, 40; Mr S. Watt, 11.

We also thank the following for kindly lending photographs during the preparation of the book, though not all could be used: Sandy Borthwick, John Craig, Robert Kenney, Robert Lister, Charles McCaig, Cathy McIlroy, Martha MacMillan, Jean Parker, Margaret Patrick, Peter Russell, Marion Smith, Margaret Suttie, and Sam Watt.